D1068240

THE CREATIVE MANAGER

Peter Russell
Roger Evans

THE CREATIVE MANAGER

Finding Inner Vision and Wisdom in Uncertain Times

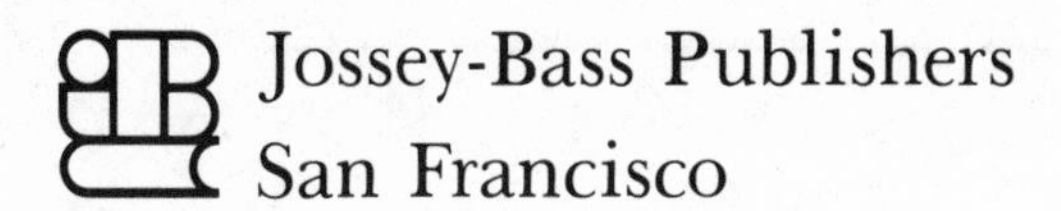

Jossey-Bass Publishers
San Francisco

For sales outside the United States contact Maxwell Macmillan International Publishing Group, 866 Third Avenue, New York, New York 10022

The paper used in this book is acid-free and meets the State of California requirements for recycled paper (50 percent recycled waste, including 10 percent postconsumer waste), which are the strictest guidelines for recycled paper currently in use in the United States.

Library of Congress Cataloging-in-Publication Data

Russell, Peter, date.
The creative manager : finding inner vision and wisdom in uncertain times / Peter Russell, Roger Evans. — 1st ed.
p. cm. — (A joint publication in the Jossey-Bass management series and the Jossey-Bass social and behavioral science series)
Includes bibliographical references (p.).
ISBN 1-55542-413-9
1. Creative ability in business. I. Evans, Roger, date. II. Title. III. Series: Jossey-Bass management series. IV. Series: Jossey-Bass social and behavioral science series.
HD53.R87 1992
658.4—dc20 91-44415
CIP

FIRST EDITION
HB Printing 10 9 8 7 6 5 4 3 2 1 *Code 9232*

A joint publication in

THE JOSSEY-BASS MANAGEMENT SERIES

and

THE JOSSEY-BASS SOCIAL AND BEHAVIORAL SCIENCE SERIES

To
Joan and Anna
for their love and support

CONTENTS

PREFACE

> Man is a prisoner of his own way of thinking and of his own stereotypes of himself.
>
> His machine for thinking, the brain, has been programmed for a vanished world.
>
> This old world was characterized by the need to manage things—stone, wood, iron.
>
> The new world is characterized by the need to manage complexity. Complexity is the very stuff of today's world.
>
> The tool for handling complexity is ORGANIZATION.
>
> But our concepts of organization belong to the much less complex old world, not to the much more complex today's world.
>
> Still less are they adequate to deal with the next epoch of complexification, in a world of explosive change.
>
> —*Stafford Beer (1975)*

We live in turbulent times. All over the world, organizations of all descriptions are facing increasingly rapid and unpredictable change. Many, however successful they appear, are in a period of profound crisis. Management practices that were successful in the past are no longer working. Leaders and managers are attempting to do the best they can under the circumstances, but it is not easy. Their initial response, like that of an individual faced with an existential crisis, has been to reach for familiar techniques and to look for ways to reorganize structures and practices. But as anyone in crisis soon finds out, attempting to resolve the issues on a superficial level alone seldom works. It is a more fundamental problem that is calling for our attention.

Those managers, and we ourselves, know in our bones that the old, tried and trusted ways of managing change are not

Note: From *Platform for Change* by Stafford Beer. (West Sussex, England: John Wiley & Sons, 1975.) Reprinted with permission of the publisher.

enough. We must find new approaches, new tools, to help us release much more of our creative potential, to face our world with a fresh outlook. Given that the future looks likely to bring even faster change and greater complexity, finding those tools has now become an imperative.

This is why fifteen years ago we began exploring the subject of creativity in a variety of corporate settings: multinational and national companies, public-sector organizations, manufacturing services, and high-tech industries. In the course of this work, we discovered that releasing individual and organizational creativity involved far more than passing along new skills and techniques and generating new ideas. Thus, we began to explore management and the creative process in greater depth. We embarked on a program in which managers at all levels could temporarily disengage from the immediacy of the issues facing them and be free, at least for a time, to consider a dimension of their lives rarely dealt with in organizational settings: their inner worlds. We encouraged them to look at their own needs, at what they really valued, at the ways in which they related to other people, at how they blocked their innate creativity, and at the processes they went through when confronted with a problem. We saw that this approach resulted in both an increase in the organization's ability to handle complex and challenging issues and an improvement in the quality of managers' personal lives.

We seemed to be breaking new ground. We began noticing that while there were several books on creativity in organizations and many on personal development, none seemed to integrate the two areas or, more important, to speak to the deeper, more fundamental issues. So we decided to gather our experiences and insights into a book.

The "Hard" Skills of Tomorrow

While *The Creative Manager* certainly deals with skills for how to manage your own creativity and that of others, it is not just another management "how-to" book. It is about something deeper: about showing you how to become more flexible in your thinking and responses; about developing new ways of dealing with the stresses you face; and about maintaining stability in the face of increasing turbulence, so that, in Gareth Morgan's words, you can "ride the waves of change." Through engaging your own creative process we set out to show you, the reader, how to manage this crucial inner dimension, in which your attitudes and values affect your thinking, your decisions, and your behavior.

Most of us do not find it easy to work at this level. Developing new skills and techniques may be something we can approach comfortably, but when it comes to managing our attitudes and beliefs, we are in uncharted territory. The inner dimensions are harder to see, harder to measure, harder to understand, and much harder to handle. Consequently, little time has been spent exploring how to actually *work* in these areas.

We believe that organizations must now take the inner lives and creative welfare of their employees very seriously. If companies are to cope with the challenges ahead, they must find ways to link the intractable demands of highly professional management with the growing need to manage the inner world of the human being. Although these inner skills are far less tangible than, say, marketing or computer skills, they are no less critical. They are the lubricant of any organization and are vital to its success. In this respect, these are the "hard" (difficult) management skills of the future.

This book attempts to describe in simple terms the mechanisms through which the subtler levels of our minds affect all aspects of our lives. It explores the roles they play in the creative process and provides ideas for how to work with them and so become more open minded. It also discusses what has happened to organizations as they began to tackle deeper inner issues.

We see this book as a beginning, a first step toward delineating the "other way" that we believe is essential if individuals and organizations are to successfully navigate the future. As much as *The Creative Manager* is a book on management, it is also a book on self-exploration – a book to set you thinking. It is an attempt to raise awareness about some of the most important issues of our time.

Who Is the Book For?

The Creative Manager is for people who are interested in developing their creative faculties and managing their world better. It is for executives who are struggling to lead their organizations forward in these uncertain times. It is for those who want a deeper understanding of the process of change and who are looking for new ways of releasing the creative potential of their employees. It is for managers who want to understand their workers more deeply and create a more empowering workplace. It is for consultants and trainers who want to find another way, who see that merely rearranging structures and sending people to training seminars does not tackle the real issues. It is for educators who want to bring deeper meaning to their work. It is also for those concerned about the social accountability of organizations in the world today.

Although this book is written largely in the context of our work in corporations, with managers in the conventional sense, it is also intended for the general reader. It draws upon what is common to us all, and is written so that we may each become creative managers of our lives.

Overview of the Contents

The first chapter presents the context of the book. It looks at creativity and the other inner qualities required to manage ever-increasing change. Chapter Two introduces the creative manager and his or her role in the world today. We see that creative managers are not themselves new, but have existed throughout history. They are characterized by their willingness to look at their times with fresh eyes and make their visions a reality. The way of these creative managers is a way based on a deeper understanding of human creativity; in this respect, it is an inner way.

Chapter Three explores this inner way. It looks in depth at

the various phases of the creative process that run throughout our lives. Many of us currently have a good understanding of managing the outer aspects of the process, but the more mysterious inner aspects of creativity are much more difficult to handle. These are the frontiers that we believe management can no longer afford to ignore. This chapter therefore provides the framework for the rest of the book.

Chapters Four and Five lay the ground for releasing creativity and discuss how crucial it is to challenge our assumptions and mindsets. This requires that we free ourselves to live in the present and shed the burden of past attitudes and beliefs.

Chapter Six looks at the increasing pressures of living in a world of accelerating change, and at how stress can limit our creativity. This chapter brings a unique dimension to the book: stress is seen here not only as a danger but also as an opportunity to discover self-mastery. For the creative manager, stress can open another door to the vastness of the inner world.

Chapter Seven shows how the new frontiers of management that we have been discussing are reflected in the dramatic changes taking place in individual values. Increased self-awareness, so important for releasing creativity, is something that more and more people are exploring. It represents yet another hidden opportunity of the information age.

In some respects, Chapter Eight is the heart of the book. It is about exploring a deeper understanding of ourselves—our needs, our visions, and our deepest motivations. It is about learning to use this greater inner awareness to manage the more mysterious aspects of the creative process. It is about listening to our own inner wisdom and putting it into action in all aspects of our lives.

In Chapter Nine we look at how creative managers are not just concerned with their inner realities: they are also men and women of action. As such, they are inevitably engaged with other people. Learning to work with others is the cornerstone of any successful organization. This final chapter concerns itself with the hard work of applying our awareness and creativity in relationships. We grapple with the questions, How can we improve the quality of our communication? What makes a creative team work? How can others be empowered to become creative managers in their own right?

The Creative Story of the Book

Writing *The Creative Manager* has been a personal journey in creativity for both of us. It began in Nigeria, where we were running a program for one of our multinational clients. For some time we had been musing on the idea of writing a book that brought together all the material that we were using in our organizational work. Having a morning free, we filled a very large sheet of paper with a detailed "mind map" of all our ideas, their structure and organization, and the underlying themes we wanted to convey.

Turning this map into a book seemed a relatively easy task. Since when we returned to England both of us became busy with our professional commitments, we enlisted the help of a journalist friend to work with us. This plan certainly got us started, but after a while we realized something was missing. The book that was developing did not really capture the vision that had so inspired us in Nigeria.

It slowly dawned on us just how difficult it was to convey our thinking to another, to transfer the underlying spirit to someone who had not lived through our years of working together. The only way to capture that spirit was to write the whole book ourselves. We began the process by each taking responsibility for the initial preparation of some of the chapters, passing them on then to the other for additions and editing.

But this did not seem to get us much further; in fact, the book seemed to be moving even more slowly. Then, in the midst of our growing frustration, the truth hit us: the book was coming not from two individual minds but from our joint thinking. When we were apart, the book had no essence, no real life; when we worked together, the inspiration returned and the book flowed out of us.

There was only one solution. We had to write together. So, taking a leave of absence from our partners, we committed our minds to the book and went away to a friend's cottage in the country.

Our country cottage provided the isolation we needed, but we were still stuck with the mindset that we had to work separately on individual chapters. Fortunately, freezing weather and a lack of space forced us closer and closer together until, after a few days, one of us had the insight: since this book is something that seems to be coming out of our joint thinking, why don't we try working together at the same computer on the same chapter?

That was when the real process of writing began. From that moment on, almost every sentence in this book was written by both of us. We set one of the Macintoshes up beside the fireplace, expanded the typeface to eighteen points, and sat back in armchairs thinking together onto the screen. In less than three months, we wrote the whole book, accomplishing far more than we had done in the previous three years.

Composing jointly on the same screen helped bring our minds together. Very often, after a period of silently studying a piece we had just written, we would utter the same words simultaneously. At other times, one of us would see something that the other would have missed. The result of this collective writing as a higher quality of text than either of us would have produced working separately.

This is not to imply that it was easy. But even in our moments of frustration, the fact that there were two of us enabled us to move beyond it much more rapidly than we would have on our own. Having jointly acknowledged our frustration, we could see whether it was time we took a break and relaxed, went for a walk, went out for a meal, or took a fresh look at what we were trying to write.

Writing as a team taught us to respect our differences in a new way. We were well acquainted with the respective roles we took when consulting or teaching together. When we were writing, however, our roles were reversed, leading us to a renewed respect for each other's strengths. The more we learned about each other, the more we were able to support both each other and the process of the book. An element crucial to the success of this approach was the fact that we shared one vision; there was unity beneath our differences.

Perhaps the greatest discovery of all concerned telling the truth. Sometimes that meant expressing our discomforts and frustrations and honoring the questions and concerns that voiced themselves; at other times it meant being willing to speak or write only what we felt to be true from our own experience. This was important for both of us. We wanted to create a book that appealed to people's inner knowing as well as to their conscious knowing. To do this, we had to be continually willing to listen to and express our own inner knowing.

To encourage this openness, we would at times ask, What does the book want to say? or, What does the book want of us at this moment? Another continual touchstone that we used was to ask, Where is life in this section? Creativity, we believe, is intrinsic to life, and for the book to reflect our vision, we wanted life to be present throughout.

Trusting also meant being open to the completely unexpected. Coincidental chains of events arising from the interplay of our thoughts sometimes led us to just the material or examples we needed (often without realizing it) at just the right time. Either of us on his own would probably have pushed on and not allowed the coincidences to unfold as they did.

None of this implies that we developed a formula to follow. The key was learning to trust: trust our inner voice, trust our feelings, trust each other, and trust our joint-mindedness.

In short, neither of us could have written this book alone. Nor could we have written it together had we not recognized that the book was coming from our collective thinking. Moreover, had we not been willing to trust the creative process in all its aspects, we certainly could not have written it together as rapidly and as satisfyingly as we did.

Acknowledgments

With a book of this nature, based on our experience with organizations and people from around the world, there are many whom we would like to thank. Without the support of Rose-

Marie Aitken, Bram Bakker, Eric Bunge, Rex Burrow, Lennart Dahlgren, Mahmoud Eboo, Ralph Edebo, Ram Gidoomal, Keith Gilchrist, Mike Hamilton, Margaret Harrison, Ton Kunneman, Henk Mylanus, Torborg Nilsson, Alex Oechslin, John Painter, Mike Payne, Annika Sandstrom, Azad Shivdasani, Agne Svanberg, Max Weeden, and Eckart Wintzen, we would have had no book to write. These were the people who invited us to work with their organization or team.

Most of the examples quoted in this book have come from individuals with whom we have worked. Since we do not refer to them by name in the text, we would like to thank them here. They are Sunder Advani, John Ajene, Hans Barth, Andrew Blake, Tony Bradburn, Peter Bregman, Captain Chadda, Dara Contractor, Tony Cornel, Björn Dahlback, Peter Dawson, Maynard Donker, Leif Elsby, Foster Gault, Freddy Ghassens, Juhan Kohl, L. Lawal, Mike Laycock, Bengt Lindgren, Pramode Metre, Bill Mills, Henry Okolo, Alabi Olaleye, V. Ramchandran, Fred Ramundo, Danielle Roex, Graham Sanderson, Hans Scholten, Tony Smith, Willy Söderberg, David Steavenson, Nico Timmerman, Alison Weller, Nicholas Wilshaw, Elisabeth Wistrand, and Jose Zwiers-Smakman.

Many friends and colleagues have contributed to our work over the years. Here we would particularly like to thank Mark Brown for his exposition of mindsets, and also Chris Bakker, Hendrik van Beek, Tony Corke, Brian Durkin, Chris Elphick, Victor Marino, John Moss-Jones, Joe Sohm, and Ian Taylor.

As we prepared the early drafts, Anuradha Vittachi was of invaluable assistance in helping us get many of our ideas out of our heads and organized into a book. And during subsequent phases of the preparation, Lisbeth Almhöjd, Cynthia Alves, Mike Brown, Jane Henry, Mark Horowitz, Anna Pauli, and Kate Vickers gave us valuable feedback and made many useful suggestions.

We are grateful to Rupert Sheldrake for providing the inkblot illustrations in Chapter Four, to Gerald Fisher for permission to use the series of drawings in Chapter Four, and to Peter Nixon for the graph in Chapter Six.

We would also like to thank Malini Hettiaratchi for being continually willing to help whenever and however needed. A big thank-you to Roger, Rita, and Ken Nutting and to David Wynne for their kindness in allowing us to use their cottages, on the wild coast of Sussex and in the depths of Suffolk, respectively, in which to hide away for three months with our Mac.

London, England Peter Russell
January 1992 Roger Evans

Much of the material about managers and organizations included in this book was obtained during our consulting, training, and personal experiences. The research is based on a combination of published accounts, our own data, personal accounts, and commonly accepted knowledge and beliefs.

THE AUTHORS

Peter Russell received a first-class honors degree (1969) from the University of Cambridge in theoretical physics and psychology, and a master's degree (1971), also from Cambridge, in computer science. He then spent three years at the University of Bristol conducting research into the psychology of meditation. Russell's books include *The Brain Book* (1978), *The Global Brain* (1983), and *The White Hole in Time* (1992). A video based on *The Global Brain* received the Swedish Public Relations Audio Visual Grand Prix and Gold Award in 1985.

Russell was one of the first people to run self-development programs in business and over the last fifteen years has been a consultant to many international corporations in the areas of stress management, mindsets, the learning process, and creative thinking. He is also interested in the long-term implications of social and technological innovation and the changes in human thinking that these require. He writes, lectures, and gives broadcasts on these subjects in both Europe and the United States.

Roger Evans is managing director of Creative Learning Consultants, a management consulting and educational group based in London. A psychotherapist with a small private practice, he is also director of the Institute of Psychosynthesis, a psychotherapy training institute in London.

He obtained his first degree (1963) from the University of London in pharmacy, and his master's degree (1968) from York University, Toronto, in business administration. He is trained as a psychotherapist and was certified through the Psychosynthesis Institute in San Francisco in 1976. He has extensive management experience, having spent the 1960s in international business in both North America and Europe.

Evans's main focus over the past ten years has been the

Evans's main focus over the past ten years has been the development of his management consulting practice, whose clients include a wide range of corporations and government agencies in the United States, Europe, Scandinavia, and Africa that are beginning to develop creative learning cultures. He is currently interested in developing long-term relations with organizations whose members want to understand the "hard" human skills of the 1990s.

Evans is particularly interested in the support and development of international projects that facilitate global collaboration and individual empowerment. In 1982, he helped found the Resource Group, a foundation fostering new perspectives in global cooperation.

THE CREATIVE MANAGER

1

The Creative Response to Change

> In a time when knowledge, constructive and destructive, is advancing by the most incredible leaps and bounds into a fantastic atomic age, genuinely creative adaptation seems to represent the only possibility that man can keep abreast of the kaleidoscopic change in his world. . . .
>
> Unless individuals, groups and nations can imagine, construct and creatively revise new ways of relating to these complex changes, the lights will go out.
>
> Unless man can make new and original adaptations to his environment as rapidly as his science can change the environment, our culture will perish. . . . Annihilation will be the price we pay for a lack of creativity.
>
> —*Carl Rogers (1954)*

Everywhere we look we see change—in technologies, scientific theories, social customs, values, organizational structures, even people. Indeed, it is often said of the current times that the only certainty is change itself.

Change, however, is nothing new; it is intrinsic to life itself. What is new is the rate at which these changes are occurring. Never before in the history of humanity have our understandings, our technologies, our customs, our values, our organizations, and people themselves changed so quickly.

If we look back just twenty years, we see a different world: a world without personal computers, satellite television, or cellular telephones; a world without the dramatic mobility and variety in jobs we have today; a world without "big bang" stock markets and global economic interdependence, which affect even the smallest companies; a world with little awareness of widespread hunger, energy shortages, and ecological devastation. If we look back one hundred years, the world is hardly recognizable: no radio, no cars, no airplanes, no electronics, no oil, no plastics, no cinema. If we look back one thousand years, we are in a different world altogether.

This trend toward ever-accelerating rates of change stretches back the length of human history. In neolithic times progress occurred over millennia; two thousand years ago it occurred over centuries. Today, radical changes can occur in one decade. Indeed, just as change itself is natural to life, so is the acceleration of change.

Much of this accelerated change has its origins in the world of technology, in which each new contribution and discovery has built upon its predecessors, pushing growth on faster. The Industrial Revolution, for example, gave birth to mass production processes and increasingly refined manufacturing technologies. Two hundred years later, when we chose to start manufacturing computers and silicon chips, we did not have to reinvent factories or the high technologies involved; they had already been established. Consequently, the Information Revolution took hold in a fraction of the time it took the Industrial Revolution to establish itself.

Moreover, the very nature of information technology means that it will evolve much faster than industrial technology. Information is much more flexible than matter. It takes many years before a steel girder design needs major modification, but software programs can and do need to change much more frequently—almost from week to week. Major software innovations such as windows and icons, once they proved their efficiency, spread through the industry very rapidly indeed. To mass produce a new software program, one needs only a single computer, not a new factory.

However giddy the speed of change may seem today, we can be sure of one thing: barring catastrophe and disaster, ten years from now the pace of life is going to be much faster than today—and another decade later, considerably faster still.

Change and the Organization

These rapid rates of change inevitably have a profound effect on organizations. Long-established corporations that have been unable to recognize or respond to changing technologies and markets have fallen by the wayside. The managers of American railroads, for example, thought the future was going to be business as normal, but they saw their customers turn to the roads and airways. The British shipbuilding, textiles, and aircraft industries are other industrial dinosaurs that were so well established on their path that they were unable to adapt fast enough when the rate of change accelerated.

New industries have started up almost overnight. Computer manufacturers, software houses, management consultants, and bioengineering companies have appeared like spring flowers. Some have survived to become household names, but many, after enjoying a rapid bloom, have quietly faded into history. Others, unable to get more than a toehold in their rapidly changing and highly competitive marketplaces, vanished before they were even noticed.

Twenty years ago, a company might have taken a year or two to deliberate major shifts in product and direction. Today, such decisions often have to be made in months—sometimes in weeks. Companies within the computer industry in particular often race to get the latest breakthrough in technology or software to the market before competitors do or hurry to catch up with their competitors' sudden surprise announcements of new products. John Sculley, president of California-based Apple Computers, is in a better position than most people to appreciate this phenomenon. In his book *Odyssey* he writes:

> Time compression has nearly crippled our ability to cope with change. Technology has made the world a smaller, faster place that penalizes the slow-moving and stable institution. Companies that can quickly get ideas and information through their organizations for discussion and action will have distinct competitive advantages over others [1987, p. 402].

Large corporations may have the advantage of greater momentum and stability and, therefore, may not be so easily swamped by change. But they also have greater inertia. Trying to change the direction of a large multinational corporation is like trying to turn a supertanker. When an iceberg suddenly looms out of the mist ahead, decisions must be made quickly if the tanker is to be turned in time. The crew of a smaller, more maneuverable craft can take a little longer to assess the situation—assuming that it is not in the supertanker's way!

This increasing pressure for quick reactions takes its toll on organizations and individuals alike. Without the time to think things through, decisions may be made more on the basis of the past than of a full appreciation of the future, and often from a state of corporate panic rather than being cool, calm, and collected.

Ironically, the very factors that demand new ways of seeing and new reponses tend to limit our flexibility. Being under pressure can lead us to feel insecure. If we must venture into unfamiliar ground while we are under pressure, our insecurity can only increase. The resulting anxiety can lead us to play it safe and become rigid in our thinking.

The growing complexity of many of the problems we face often means that no one individual has all the information and perspectives needed to make the best decision. Yet we often see asking for help as a weakness rather than a strength. When we fail to cope on our own, we may interpret our failure as a personal inadequacy. In some people, this can lead to defensiveness, dogmatism, and an authoritarian style; in others, it leads to feelings of helplessness, depression, and withdrawal—hardly the best states of mind for dealing with the demands of rapid change. It is little wonder, then, that so many of the decisions we make turn out to be shortsighted, inappropriate, incomplete, or just plain wrong.

In his valedictory speech in 1986 as retiring chairman of the Confederation of British Industries, Sir Terence Beckett decried the damage done to business by "short-termism":

> We have to recognize that decisions in industry taken today will produce repercussions lasting not just through the next season or the next year, but throughout the next twenty

> or thirty years. Snap decisions made in the heat of a single moment can affect a business for decades [Beckett, 1986].

At the same time that organizations are feeling the pressure to make fast, expedient decisions, the growing interconnectedness and complexity of world affairs requires us to explore the long-term implications of these decisions. Since this in-depth thinking takes more time, a conflict frequently arises between the pressures for a quick decision and the need for a good decision.

Short-term problems always seem more urgent—that is their nature. Long-term needs, on the other hand, can always be put off for a little while. If, for example, its finances are squeezed, an organizaiton views research and development, training, social programs, and other long-term investments as expenses that can be cut back with little noticeable effect; they are always the ones that can wait.

This applies to many other organizations, not just to corporations. In the 1980s, governments in the United Kingdom, the United States, and some of the other developed countries reacted to short-term economic pressures by cutting back on education, scientific research, health care, and social services. This approach may well be valid from the short- and medium-term financial and political perspective, but whether or not it makes sense for the long-term health of a nation remains to be seen. We do not mean to imply that the long-term perspective is necessarily the correct one (if short-term needs are not taken into account, there may well be no long-term future) but rather to highlight the very real difficulties that face organizations as they try to balance these seemingly conflicting needs.

Change and the Individual

Change can be exciting and stimulating. It can trigger new ideas, fire us with enthusiasm, provide us with new opportunities, confront us with new challenges, and awaken us from our slumbers. Change can be the spice of life.

Yet it also brings uncertainty, and in doing so seems to bring us as individuals many problems. Economic changes bring changes in employment and the threat of redundancy. New technologies bring new processes and more things to learn. Scientific discoveries bring new ways of thinking, challenging us to let go of cherished beliefs. Social changes may threaten our established identity. Personal changes may affect our values, leading us to question ourselves as to what is right and what is really important.

And there are long-term uncertainties: What will the world be like in twenty or forty years' time? Will we still be here? Will we survive the threat of nuclear annihilation? Will the world's economy collapse? Will all the pressures associated with a rapidly changing world lead to totalitarian states in which individuals are coerced into conformity through a multitude of technologies? Or will the future be more like the one of William Gibson's novels, in which cybernetic and genetic technologies run amok, brain implants flash the time in front of our eyes, computers battle to defeat each other's "viruses," and we eat "factory-grown" meat? Or will some "new age" vision come to pass, in which wisdom and enlightenment prevail, allowing us to clean up the mess we have made, live in harmony with ourselves and all life, and manage our future with intelligence and care? The truth is, no one knows—although many have their beliefs.

The future may even be one that none of us have yet imagined. John Harvey-Jones, former chairman of the British chemical giant ICI, writes in his recent book on leadership, *Making It Happen*:

> It has to be possible to dream and speak the unthinkable, for the only thing we do know is that we shall not know what tomorrow's world will be like. It will have changed more than even the most outrageous thinking is likely to encompass [1988, p. 39].

Whatever may or may not happen, the very uncertainty of the future promotes anxiety. We begin wondering: What will happen to me, my family, my pension, my way of life, my health? What can I do about the future? Will I be able to cope with it?

Nor is it just the future implications of change that bother us. The faster things change, the faster we have to adapt, and the greater the pressures upon us. Take electronic mail, for example. In many contemporary high-tech companies, all employees are linked together through their computer terminals. Instead of sending a letter or memo and receiving a reply a few days later, a person can send a message across the world, either from a keyboard or by voice, and receive a response within hours or minutes.

These rapid communication systems clearly are very efficient, but they have hidden human costs. They give us no time to breathe. We may be pressured to make decisions before we have all the facts or explore the alternatives. Our level of personal contact may be reduced. And we face mounting pressures to access, digest, and respond to increasing amounts of information. For example, managers at seminars rush off at the first break to the nearest computer terminal to check whether or not their office has left a message. They are not always eagerly awaiting a message—often they are relieved to find there are none—but because such instant communication is possible, they no longer have any excuse for not receiving and responding to messages. Thus, people are increasingly expected to behave like the computers they use, rather than like the human beings who use them.

Computers, fax machines, portable stock-quote machines, voice mail, and portable phones have all vastly increased the speed at which communication occurs and business is transacted. Tony Schwartz (1988), writing in *Vanity Fair*, describes this "acceleration syndrome" as

> . . . a state of constant overdrive. There's more information than ever to absorb, more demands to meet, more roles to play, the technology to accomplish everything faster, and never enough time to get it all done.

> The phenomenon is most visible, of course, among those in fast-paced professions—communications, politics, Wall Street, and Hollywood—and in big cities that are themselves intense, especially New York and Los Angeles. But living at an accelerated pace isn't limited to major metropolises and high-powered professionals. Clerical workers who use computers, for example, report with increasing frequency that they find themselves adapting their own rhythms to those of the computer. For that matter, just ask any working mother and father, no matter how placid their temperament or high their income, whether they find themselves running faster to try to accomplish more and yet struggling constantly to keep up.

The faster change comes and the less able we are to cope with it, the more vulnerable we are to stress. We each have limits to how much pressure we can take, whether it be physical, mental, or emotional, without showing signs of strain.

The cost to industry of stress-related disorders is enormous. In the United States, as many as 100 million working days per year and billions of dollars are lost because of workers' backaches, headaches, nervous tension, and exhaustion. In European countries, the estimated cost is very similar, proportional to the population. If we include health problems that are exacerbated by stress, such as colds, the cost is much higher still.

The cost of employee health problems, however, is not the major stress-related problem for organizations. The cost of mistakes and poor decisions made by people under stress can be many times greater. Stress also affects our relationships with one another. When we feel stressed, we do not give each other much time or attention, we too easily get annoyed or impatient with people who do not do what we want, and we generally communicate less well. The result is misunderstanding and frustration.

As the pace of life continues to accelerate, stress is clearly going to become more and more of a problem. Social commentators such as Alvin Toffler have repeatedly pointed out that if we are to survive the future, we must develop our powers of adaptation. We must become more flexible and see change as less of a threat. We must learn to ride the waves of change rather than become swamped by them. Change will not go away. Our challenge is not to restrain it, but to respond to it in new ways, to be able to cope with the totally unexpected when it suddenly arrives.

Change and Society

The rapid acceleration in the pace of life is also having a severe impact on the world around us. The hunger of industrial society for energy and resources and the unprecedented amounts of waste we produce are already having major consequences for the world in which we live. In the future, the ecological repercussions of our avarice will almost certainly become more alarming and will have widespread social and political implications. Although most organizations study economic and market forecasts in great detail, few take into account the fact that social, political, and ecological change can shatter the most sophisticated forecast. The demands of pressure groups and an increasingly concerned and vocal general public are the very tools that render organizations most vulnerable. Responding to these unprecedented and unforeseeable changes in our environment is going to become a major task for the members of every organization.

These problems cannot be ignored. Our growing global interdependence and the near-instant speed of communication have brought us face-to-face with the crises confronting us. Moreover, the size and complexity of these problems can, all too easily, leave us feeling overwhelmed, frightened, and powerless. We seem to be in the midst of a massive societal breakdown, hurtling at breakneck speed toward disaster, with nothing we can do to stop it.

Yet, deep inside, many people know that the individual, and only the individual, can change things. Whether they have been political leaders who have had a vision, scientists who have had a new idea, artists who have expressed the spirit of the times, journalists who have fought for a cause, managers who have pushed through new practices, or teachers who have inspired others, individuals have always been the instigators of change.

Clearly, a single individual cannot solve all the problems of our world. Nevertheless, we each can make changes within our own workplaces, communities, or families. Our responsibility is to develop creative ways of thinking and acting that make the best possible use of the many opportunities presented by the constant change and innovation of our present-day world. No one has responsibility for the entire organization; yet the more people who take responsibility for themselves and their immediate sphere of influence, the more the organization itself can change.

We do not lack the power to contribute; what we lack is the knowledge of *how* to exercise our power—and the *courage* to do so. We lack empowerment.

How can we gain empowerment? How can we bring more courage and vision into our lives? How can we make more of a contribution to the organizations and societies to which we belong? How can we manage our world with greater creativity? These questions are the focus of this book.

Coping with Change Through Stability and Flexibility

A key ingredient in our response to change must be inner stability. Riding the waves of change is like sailing a boat through stormy seas. The wind pulls so strongly on the sails that we are in danger of keeling over. Yet, if we do not sail close to the wind, we will be awash with mountainous seas. We are all sailors in this sea, facing the forces of unpredictable times, trying to steer ourselves and the craft we have created through increasing turbulence.

Sailors in rough seas need great skill and understanding. They also need to maintain an inner calm. Most of us would rather sail with the sailor who has a deep understanding of his or her own capacities and limitations and an inner resource of calm and peace than with one who only knows techniques for handling a boat. We know that in the face of complexity, uncertainty, and confusion, inner stability is essential. It allows us to respond naturally without overreacting; it tells us when to relax and sit back and when to be active and dynamic.

At this time in history, humanity is sailing into a very fierce storm indeed. No one knows what the future will bring, but it is certain that we will face changes on a scale never experienced before. When they come, they are almost certain to be sudden and unexpected. One of the most pressing needs of our time is for us to become more at peace with ourselves, to find a still center of inner stability and calm from which we can think and act with greater clarity and creativity. Our challenge is not to prophesy how the future will be or to try to keep change under control but to respond creatively to the unforeseen when it appears. This requires an open mind.

We must be able to let go of old perceptions, attitudes, and ways of seeing and take on the new with the freshness, vitality, and freedom it demands of us. We must be prepared to question all our assumptions concerning who we are, where we are heading, what we really need, and what is most important to us.

Clearly, those organizations and individuals most likely to survive the coming changes will be those that are the most flexible and adaptable. We need to rise above the rigid thinking and fixed views that tend to trap us. While they may have served us in the past, they may all too easily restrict our perception of the present and the future. As Gareth Morgan writes in *Riding the Waves of Change*,

> We are facing a future where we will see changes all the time. How do we organize our corporations to face change? How do we get that through to people? It's not just a communications exercise, it's a mindset, it's a different way of thinking [1988, p. 54].

The need for inner flexibility does not conflict with the need for inner stability; each depends upon the other. If we cannot maintain an inner calm, we may find ourselves clinging to set patterns of behavior for a sense of security. On the other hand, if we are at peace within, we are much freer to respond to change and to respond more appropriately. Being flexible does not mean being blown hither and thither by the winds of change. When we are truly flexible, we are like a tree in the wind: anchored firmly by its roots yet able to bend with the storm.

Change and the Creative Manager

Stability and flexibility not only are two key ingredients in the management of change but also are intrinsic to creativity. The creative person is not panicked by new situations and challenges, but can step back and look at them with fresh eyes. To manage the future successfully requires new thinking and a willingness to look at new responses. The unprecedented changes that humanity will undergo as we move through the 1990s and into the first decades of the twenty-first century will demand that we draw upon our creative resources as never before.

We can be masters of our own destiny. But to use that mastery wisely, we must draw deeply upon the creative spirit that lives within us all. We must become conscious creators of our future, steering ourselves carefully through the turbulent seas ahead. We must learn to manage our future with inner stability, flexibility, and deep creativity.

This book is about drawing upon that well of creativity and using it to empower ourselves and those around us. It is not just about understanding creativity; it is about understanding ourselves and life and about allowing the creativity within to infuse our life, for creativity is intrinsic to life.

This book is also about us as managers—and not just those of us normally labeled as managers. The term *management*, in its most general sense, may be defined as "the optimization of resources." In this respect, we are all managers. We are all seeking to optimize the resources available to us. Whether we are managing staff in a company, managing a production line, managing financial resources, managing a farm, managing a home, managing our relationships, managing our lives, or managing our inner selves, we are managing, in one way or another, practically all of the time.

Management is part of being human. Humans, unlike other creatures, have hands (*manus*) with fully opposable thumbs. We can handle the world in which we live, and through our hands our creativity can take shape. We can make tools and with these tools make changes far beyond those created by any other creature. Yet our extraordinary creative power requires that we use it with wisdom and care. We must allow our creativity to flow through us, and from us into the world, so that we can channel it for the highest good.

2

Who Is the Creative Manager?

Life is making us abandon established stereotypes and outdated views. It is making us discard illusions. The very concept of the nature and criteria of progress is changing. It would be naive to think that the problems plaguing mankind today can be solved with means and methods which were applied or seemed to work in the past. . . .

Today we face a different world for which we must seek a different road to the future. In seeking it, we must, of course, draw upon the accumulated experience and yet be aware of the fundamental differences between the situation yesterday and what we are facing today.

—Mikhail Gorbachev (1988)

Becoming a more creative manager is not just a matter of practicing new techniques and methodologies, although these may certainly help. It also involves becoming more aware of our own inner processes, adopting a new style of thinking and perceiving, and learning to see ourselves and our problems in a new way.

As suggested in the previous chapter, some of the most demanding and critical problems confronting managers in the years to come—whether they be managers of a nation, a small community, or a business—will be those that stem from the global repercussions of contemporary civilization. We will not solve these problems through using techniques and methodologies alone. The roots of these problems run deep into our culture, and mustering the creativity needed to solve them will require us to think in new ways about our world and about ourselves.

The challenges ahead are very real and cannot be ignored. We have much to fear and much to take care of if we are to steer a safe course through these turbulent times. But perhaps the greatest danger of all is not seeing what lies behind these many threats and reacting only to the surface issues. If we only focus on managing the world around us, we are failing to see the deep challenge facing us. We are failing to recognize that behind the environmental, economic, and social crises that we face lies an inner crisis.

If we are to manage our future with wisdom, we need to ask ourselves some searching questions: What is it in our thinking, our values, and our attitudes that leads us to respond to change in such a way that gives rise to all these problems in the first place? What is it in our thinking that leads us to manufacture a thousand times the quantity of nuclear weapons required to eliminate ourselves completely? What is it in our values that allows the rich nations to keep mountains of surplus food while millions of people are starving? What is it in our attitudes that allows us to continue to destroy the rain forests, the lungs of the planet?

A martian visiting our world for the first time might well be excused for concluding that humanity is insane. Yet, as individuals, we know that none of us intentionally set out to damage ourselves and our environment. Our own thinking appears rational, our own values appear acceptable, and our perceptions, understandable. And yet our world continues to be in crisis.

Often, our natural reaction is to look outside ourselves and to blame others for this state of affairs. But are those people we blame any different from ourselves? It is not that anyone is deliberately trying to destroy the world; we are each trying to make our own world work, and we each have limitations.

Our limitations are seldom outer ones. What holds us back today (at least those of us in the rich, developed world) are limitations in ourselves. Our real challenge is to discover what in us allows us to continue to behave in inappropriate ways.

Millions of ordinary people know that there must be a better way to manage their lives and are seeking to discover it. They are beginning to think differently about the world and about themselves. They no longer accept the idea that they have to live like leaves tossed on the sea of change. These are the people symbolized by the term *creative manager*.

Creative managers are people who are learning to think in a new way. They see the potential for learning in each moment. Rather than blaming the world and other people for creating difficulties, creative managers ask themselves, What am I learning from this? Having such an attitude is not always easy, but creative managers recognize that being open to learning is fundamental to life.

They recognize that our world demands of us increasing inner stability, a growing flexibility, and a willingness to live with uncertainty. They are aware that these attitudes are essential to a deep understanding of the creative process.

The skills of thinking, learning, and creativity are what John Naisbitt and Patricia Aburdene, in *Re-Inventing the Corporation* (1985), call the new "TLC." They do not mean what we usually think of as TLC—tender, loving care—but rather a "shorthand for learning how to *Think*, learning how to *Learn*, and learning how to *Create*. These are the new basics, the three Rs of the new information society" (p. 141).

Outwardly, creative managers may not appear to be different from any other person. They will come from different backgrounds and training and be found in every sphere of activity at work and at home. They can be recognized not by what they do but by how they approach what they do. The difference is an inner one; it is a difference of attitude.

The Creative Manager in History

The creative manager is not a new phonomenon. Throughout history, some men and women, in responding to the difficulties of their times, have been willing to step back and challenge old ways of seeing and thinking. They were people with a vision of a new and better world who dedicated themselves to making that vision a reality.

The Industrial Revolution was fathered by creative managers. The scientists and engineers who pioneered the new technologies of the time—James Watt, Josiah Wedgwood, Matthew Boulton, Erasmus Darwin, Joseph Priestley, William Withering, and others—saw the potential that they held in their grasp. They had a vision of a new world: a world in which the steam engine replaced human muscle, factories were freed from their dependence on waterpower, earthenware pipes transformed public sanitation, transportation was revolutionized by turnpikes and canals, the mechanical telegraph dramatically enhanced communication, and people could be released from the hardship of working on the land eighteen hours a day.

Empowered by their vision of how, in just a few decades, the quality of life could be significantly enhanced, these people decided to pool their energy and help each other turn their vision into reality. They founded the now almost legendary Lunar Society of Birmingham. Meeting once a month and corresponding regularly, they sought solutions to the social, political, economic, scientific, and technological problems of an industrializing community. The Industrial Revolution was no accident; it was consciously created and managed. These people knew how to tap the inherent creativity within themselves and empower one another.

At the same time, other creative managers were busy forming a new nation. The Founding Fathers of the United States of America—James Madison, Gouverneur Morris, Alexander Hamilton, Benjamin Franklin (a visiting member of the Lunar Society), George Washington, James Wilson—also had a vision of a new world. They wished to free themselves from the outdated political thinking of Europe and have a government that served the people, rather than vice versa.

Studying every political system in history and drawing on the current "leading edge" ideas of people such as Thomas Paine and Thomas Jefferson, they produced one of the most creative management documents ever written—the American Constitution. In doing so, they created a new political system that set the stage for two centuries of growth and freedom.

The birth of the United States in many ways symbolized the birth of future thinking. The founders of the United States believed that tomorrow could be better than yesterday. This was a significant break from past ways of thinking, for the European monarchies, linked by bloodlines to the past, viewed the world of yesterday as the golden age.

In Europe a hundred years earlier, the "scientific revolution" had been heralded by another group of visionaries. Doctors and philosophers such as Robert Boyle, Sir Robert Murray, John Wallis, and John Wilkins, who were interested in the emerging sciences of physics, medicine, mathematics, and astronomy, met regularly in London to share ideas and help each other in their research. Foreseeing the implications of this "new experimental philosophy," they formed what was called the Invisible College. Out of this group was later born the Royal Society of London for Improving Knowledge, more often known simply as the Royal Society, which for three centuries remained one of the most prestigious scientific institutions in the Western world.

Creative managers have been at work in all cultures throughout history, although their names may not be as well known as those of the people mentioned here. The issues they were responding to and the problems they encountered may have been very different, but these individuals knew that they could make the world a better place in which to live. They recognized that the time they lived in demanded new ways of thinking and seeing, and they used the opportunities available to them to manifest their vision.

The Creative Manager Today

Today we face new challenges. Our ever-accelerating rate of change is putting unprecedented pressures on people, organizations, and the environment. Never before have we had to deal with problems of such complexity and on such a global scale—problems that threaten the future of our species.

Once more, we are being asked to step back and look at our situation in new ways. And again, a new vision is emerging: a world healed of its insanity. In all cultures, there are people who seek to contribute to the creation of a better world. They express the emerging values of our times, rather than the values by which they have lived in the past.

In the days of the Lunar Society, the challenge was to develop and disseminate the "freedoms" inherent in the new engineering. The founders of the United States faced the challenge of building a new land of political and spiritual freedom. Today, our challenge is to manage the awesome power of our own new technologies.

How technology is used, whether or not it is used for the benefit of humanity and the living world as a whole, is controlled largely by governments and businesses. Of these two, businesses probably have the greatest worldwide influence. The impact of corporations such as IBM, Sony, BASF, Ford, Coca-Cola, Nestlé, Boeing, Levi Strauss, BBC, Heineken, Nikon, McDonald's, Shell, Mitsubishi, Unilever, Saatchi & Saatchi, Price Waterhouse, Siemens, Johnson & Johnson, Avis, and Disney can be seen and felt in almost every corner of the globe. Although some people may see the power and influence of these corporations as a great danger, they also present us with unrealized opportunities. Marjorie Kelly, editor and publisher of *Business Ethics*, suggests that business may be the last, best hope for planet Earth.

> If business has the power to destroy the Earth, might it also have the power to heal it? If business has the ability to ruin human lives, might it also have the ability to save them?
>
> The answer may be yes. From many sectors—inside and outside the corporation, among academics, activists and new thinkers—there are signs that a new life-affirming paradigm is emerging for business. Just as physics is shifting paradigms of the physical world from matter to energy, and as medicine is shifting paradigms of health care from treatment to prevention, so too is a shift underway in business. . . . The new paradigm has to do, in short, with making a better world—and using business as a tool.
>
> No, the millennium has not arrived. But there are signs that the way we think about business—and the way business thinks about itself—are beginning to change [Kelly, 1989, p. 54].

Power to the People

We should not forget that organizations are and always have been composed of people. It is people who make the judgments and decisions that determine the direction and actions of an organization. What we have to look at are the beliefs, attitudes, and values behind the judgments and decisions.

Most corporate organizations evolved in response to commercial interests, and the people who worked within them made decisions largely in the context of those interests. They asked themselves: What products have the most market potential? What will bring the best return on investment? What is in the long-term interest of the business? Such criteria were primarily financial and did not include the wider environment beyond the organization's immediate field of operation and the interests of its shareholders.

Today, however, the values and criteria that determine corporate direction are beginning to change. People are recognizing that they can no longer make business decisions in isolation from their societal implications. To be satisfied in their work, employees want more of their personal needs fulfilled than just the need for money and security. Growing numbers of people do not wish to work in jobs that cause hardship or suffering to others. We are beginning to recognize that if we do not take into account the long-term environmental consequences of our decisions, there may be no marketplace, no corporations, and no work in a decade or two.

At the same time, the power in organizations is becoming more widely distributed. In the past, a few people could be relied on to make most of the decisions, but the complexity of contemporary organizations demands that more and more people be involved in decision making. People's desire to be heard, recognized, and involved has led to open management styles. In addition, the structures of organizations are changing; hierarchies are becoming flatter and more flexible, often giving way to matrix and network structures. The net effect is that more and more people are having a direct say in the direction and activities of the organizations in which they are involved.

Thus the new values that are being expressed at an individual level are finding increasing opportunity for expression within organizations. And the far-reaching impact that organizations have on the world amplifies the opportunity for these growing values to find expression on a global level.

The creative managers of the past were fortunate enough to have the position and circumstances to be able to manifest their vision. Today, organizations are offering a similar potential leverage to many people working within them. They are becoming the vehicle through which people can express their values and vision.

A New Role for the Organization

One area in which changing personal values are beginning to have a significant impact on corporate policies is ecology. Environmental disaster is clearly not in the long-term interest of any company, yet the threat of it is so far removed from the considerations of marketing policy, annual budgets, and corporate strategy that it rarely, if ever, enters boardroom discussions. Although environmental disaster may not be an issue that is put on the table, it is an issue that is frequently in people's minds—from the boardroom to the shop floor. Few of us can notice the dangers we face without being concerned.

The chemical industry, in particular, is beset by the conflict between company policy and personal concerns. By its very nature, the industry is not very "friendly" to the environment. Chemical companies may produce toxic effluents and use dangerous processes. The products they make may have to be handled and transported carefully, may be dangerous to living systems, and may not degrade easily once their job is done.

What happens when the people working for a chemical company feel, as many people do, a responsibility toward the environment? For the company to survive financially, people may have to respond in ways that are not always in the best interests of the environment as a whole, and at the same time, the workers may have a need to see their inner values reflected in their work life. One might argue that people who find themselves in this situation should leave and find work in a more compatible industry. But for most people, this option is not practical: personal and family needs do not allow them the flexibility of retraining, they would probably have to suffer an unacceptable reduction in salary, and relocation would probably severely disrupt their family life.

An international chemical group with whom we were working found themselves faced with this conflict. A number of the employees, including some of the directors, wished to see the company adopt a policy of "environmentally friendly chemisty." They wanted the company to produce only products for water-based systems—products that were safe for the environment, the user, the public, and the employee. And they wanted these products to be produced by safe means. They believed that their company should adopt the goal of becoming, within five years, one of the cleanest chemcial companies in the world. Other members of the company, including the financial director, felt that these objectives were impractical, to say the least. These people argued that to attempt such a shift, given the current state of the industry as a whole, would be financial and hence corporate suicide.

The situation reached a crisis point at the annual strategy meeting. Feelings were running high in both camps, and people were becoming increasingly entrenched in their positions. Rather than try to resolve the polarization by argument and debate, we invited both sides to explore together their different perceptions of the issue, including the advantages and disadvantages of the two proposals. This approach allowed both sides to step back from their position without feeling that they were giving in and enabled them to hear each other's concerns.

After a day of intense exploration, the people on both sides reached some common ground. Everyone in the room, from the president to union leaders, agreed that on a personal level, they were not completely happy working in an industry that had negative environmental side effects. The conflict now had a larger context within which it could be explored and one that did not leave people polarized. The "pragmatists" were able to acknowledge the values and needs of the individual. And the "environmentalists," feeling heard, were in turn able to hear the very real concerns of the pragmatists. The conflict between the needs of the individual and the needs of the company was now a conflict everyone could understand.

It then took only a matter of hours for both sides to agree upon a workable strategy. As a consequence, within one year, the organization's plants made significant reductions in emissions, reductions beyond those likely to be required by law. New research into more acceptable products is underway. Internal safety standards have been significantly improved. And, perhaps most important as far as the long-term alignment of corporate and individual objectives is concerned, a companywide environmental education program has been established. Although participation is on a voluntary basis and the program is held outside work hours over a three-month period, 60 percent of the total work force has participated in this program.

Sustainable Development

It is not just the "dirtier" industries that are beginning to include global and environmental issues within their long-term strategies. One of the largest computer manufacturers recently took significant strides in this direction by looking at its responsibilities toward the rest of the world. The company is recognizing that business "operates only with a license from society" and that, in addition to its duties to its stakeholders, the company has real responsibilities to the community at large, including the protection of the environment at local, national, and global levels. This new thinking comes not just from a corporate need but also reflects the thinking of people within the organization. As the chief executive said in announcing the company's major support initiative for the United Nations Environmental Program:

> As a parent I have reflected on the sort of world my teenage son might live in when he's my age. . . . Will it be the better, richer world that many statesmen and industrialists promise, when they marvel about man's achievements in technology, space or medicine?
>
> Or will it be an infinitely poorer world: poorer in

> terms of pollution, literacy, urban disorganization; a world of continuing poverty?
>
> Will it be a world where peace can prevail, when the requirements of an exploding population exceed the scarce resources of water, food and housing caused by rising sea levels?
>
> Will it be a world where we are forced to shelter from a lethal sun, unprotected by the ozone layer? Will it be a world whose economic system is in total chaos caused by the climatic changes?
>
> Questions like these were regarded as alarmism in the sixties and seventies. They have become the realism of the eighties. Surely they must become the inspiration of the nineties.

Looking to the future, a growing number of companies are also beginning to appreciate that the notion of *growth* that has fueled corporations for years is now dangerously out of date. This notion limits our considerations to the physical dimensions of the economic system; that is, to an increase in economic output. But as the Club of Rome made clear twenty years ago, such growth has limits. Growth is always limited by the amount of resources available and by the environment's ability to assimilate waste. As a result, all natural growth eventually tapers off.

Today, we need to replace the notion of growth with that of *sustainable development*—*development* being defined as "a pattern of social and structural economic transformations; a continuing *qualitative* improvement in a quantitatively nongrowing economic system." We as individuals develop in a similar way. Our physical growth tapers off (usually before we reach seven feet), but our development as a person does not stop there; most of us continue to improve qualitatively—we grow inwardly. Some corporations are beginning to recognize that the same transition must now occur with humanity as a whole. To managers who worship the idol of growth, this idea comes as unpalatable news.

Social Responsibility

In the past, businesses and local communities have often been in conflict. Images still persist of the companies exploiting the local work force, while businesses felt that communities were impeding their growth. Nowadays, however, businesses increasingly are being asked, and could eventually be required by law, to play a major role in the well-being and development of local communities by supporting community initiatives with money, time, and people.

Most large corporations allocate part of their funds to charitable causes, but others go a lot further. Some have revived the old idea of tithing, or giving part of their profits for the benefit of the community. Traditionally, this part was one-tenth (which is what the word *tithe* means in Saxon English). Today, however, companies can tithe any amount, from a fraction of 1 percent to as much as 20 percent of their profits. An American confectionary company, for instance, donates more than 10 percent of its profits to local hospitals, schools, and other community services, including help for the homeless and for people who suffer from AIDS.

Anita Roddick, founder of the very successful international chain, The Body Shop, sees support of the community as a crucial element in the success of her company:

> We have discovered that our customers believe what we say, and that is one hell of a responsibility. You wear that responsibility more than you wear anything. What you do with it is to say "How can I effect change for the better?" We try by bringing attention to such things as cruelty against animals. . . and how the environment is being abused.
>
> I don't say we have found the answer. Every time we think we've reached perfection, the goalposts change. It's the searching for a better way that gives our company a stronger morale, a better purpose.

Those people who see corporations only as self-preserving financial entities out to maximize profit at others' expense often are amazed when they first hear of companies that make changes to benefit our society. But there are two things we should remember.

First, it is not the abstract entity of "the company" that has instigated these changes. The changes were begun by individuals within the company who wanted to see their values expressed. These people, in most cases, had to work hard to convince others that their proposals were indeed in the long-term interests of the business. Only then does the organization back such a proposal. As the manager in charge of the sustainable development program in a major multinational corporation remarked, "Yes, such programs are certainly good for our public relations *and* they are also in line with what the world needs, and with what I need as an individual."

The second thing we should remember is that it is not "amazing" that these changes should be taking place through organizations; it is a sign of the times.

People Matter Most

As growing numbers of people begin to express their human, social, and environmental concerns, many managers find themselves struggling to cope. In the words of Tom Peters, "Business ain't an abstraction. It is blood-and-guts human beings trying to figure out what makes somebody happy. We don't teach the value of that in our business schools."

We need a deep understanding of the people with whom we work, be they subordinates, colleagues, or bosses. Even twenty years ago, people were still regarded as an ingredient in production, as simply another cost. Managers may have given lip service to the idea that people matter most, but that service ended at the lips; very few ever acted upon the idea. They always had too many other important things to do, and, more significantly, they always had easier tasks to tackle than dealing with human beings. But in today's work environment, it is becoming increasingly important for us to understand the human side of the equation, and to a depth never imagined in the past.

This shift in attitudes is brought out clearly by Francis

Kinsman in his book *The New Agenda* (1983). He visited thirty chief executives of major British companies and management commentators and asked them one question: what do you imagine will be the most important social issues facing British management by 1990? They were given the assurance that no comments would ever be attributed to them personally, which allowed them to speak their minds without fear of judgment from colleagues, staff, or the general public.

Two issues relating to management development and training came up time and time again. One, as might be expected, was the need for skills in information technology. The other was skills with people. Moreover, people skills were seen to be more important in the long term than information skills. As one captain of industry put it:

> In the good old bad old days, people used to talk about maximization of profit; then they toned it down to optimization of profit. . . . Now you just can't get away with talking of profit unless it is in the context of every dimension of the human factor. . . . Organizations must have a wider amalgam of talent at the top—and increasingly that will mean people who understand people in all their aspects [Kinsman, 1983, p. 7].

Or as another said:

> There has to be some kind of educational process bringing the art of living into day-to-day management. There has always been a complete difference between the way individuals relate to their colleagues in business and the way that they relate to their friends and family. In the latter area, kindness, tolerance, etc., are not regarded as sentimental and wet, but as making the relationship work. Can one parallel this in business now? The difference between the two sets of attitudes is beginning to narrow and that may be the answer to tomorrow's problems [Kinsman, 1985, p. 122].

Employees in organizations are no longer content to be treated as lumps of flesh with time to sell. They are demanding to be treated as human beings with similar human needs as their bosses. This is leading to new corporate structures, less authoritarian control, increased decentralization, and more delegation of responsibilities. The divisional manager of a medium-sized corporation put it in these words:

> Our hierarchies were unquestioned in the past, but times are different now; people are more educated, beginning to say, my needs are important too. That has changed our company in a fundamental way. The organizational structure is more human, and the personnel department has become one of the most important support systems in the organization.

In our own work with corporate leaders in Europe, North America, Scandinavia, West Africa, and India, we see many managers who are passionate in their desire to see growth in their people as well as in their profits. They know that the corporation will not be successful in handling the future unless untapped human resources are released, personal conflicts are understood and resolved, and people are empowered to make a real contribution. These leaders clearly have a vision of the future but often are unsure of how to make their vision a reality. They find their past experience and training has not adequately equipped them for these new challenges.

This is how the director of the management training institute of a Scandinavian bank described this difficulty:

> We know we have to equip our leaders for the future, but even though we know this and have started a development program towards this end, there is a whole new dimension of working with people that we do not yet understand. When we can, we will then be helping people learn about themselves as people as well as learning how to manage.

Thus, the key tasks facing the leaders of the future are to create a culture that will empower people, to learn how to acknowledge and accept individual differences, and to facilitate the development of creative relationships within their organizations.

Empowerment is often seen as something one person can do for another person, but we shall see in a later chapter that this is not so. People are empowered by an environment that gives them the freedom to express themselves as fully as they can. The leader of the future must create such an environment, which will enable others to become creative managers in their own right.

Creative managers value people whose ways of thinking are contrary to their own. They know that each person brings different knowledge, experience, skills, attitudes, perceptions, and abilities to a task and that the best solutions draw upon the interplay of our individual wisdoms.

We know that we need other people and that we need to learn how to relate better to others, and yet many of us find relating to others one of the most difficult tasks in our lives. Most of us, particularly men, struggle with issues around intimacy. We have learned to interact with people mainly on an external level and have often hidden away the inner dimensions of our life. We need to listen better to others and to learn to listen to ourselves—to hear what we are really trying to say, to communicate our hopes and anxieties. The more we share our inner world and our caring nature, the more we facilitate our working together and our own empowerment.

The Illusion of Managing Change

Organizations worldwide are beginning to realize that a key ingredient in responding to change is the development of people and their creativity. Many managers who have been trained to think of organizations as machines are realizing that this view is outdated and that organizations need to be considered as living systems. Managing change in these living systems demands a radically different approach than that of managing change in a machine.

In attempting to respond to change, we tend to focus on managing its outer forms. Thus, faced with new problems, we try new problem-solving techniques. As the problems we face become more complex, we expand our computer facilities. If we feel the pressures of time mounting, we take up time management programs. To control and handle change, we go to courses that teach us to plan better, become more efficient, and develop better communication skills. It is not that these "outer" skills will not be useful; on the contrary, they are essential. However, unless the context within which they are used changes, they will only partially work.

We respond to change as if it is "out there" and as though all of our attention should be focused outside of ourselves. We respond in this way because we understand much more about managing the outer world. We are rather like the wise fool Nasrudin in the following Sufi tale:

> A neighbor found Nasrudin down on his knees looking for something.
>
> "What have you lost?" he asked.
>
> "My key," said Nasrudin.
>
> The other man got down on his knees and began searching with him. After a few minutes he asked, "Where did you drop it?"
>
> "In the house."
>
> "Then why, for heaven's sake, are you looking for it here?"
>
> "There is more light here."

This is far more than simply an amusing story; it contains a lot of human truth. The key to many contemporary issues lies within us, "at home." We have lost sight of this fact, and rather than look inside, which for many of us is dim and uncharted territory, we look for answers where "there is more light," in the more manageable world outside. Similarly, if we are to find the answers to the problems now confronting us, we must also look to the area from which they have sprung—our thinking, attitudes, and perceptions. So long as we are caught in the illusion that we can manage change by managing the world around us, we will still feel overwhelmed and powerless, and we will continue to resist change.

When new developments seem to threaten our established way of life, we can be remarkably skillful at resisting them. It is as if we had a built-in program designed to maintain the status quo. It is not that change is resisted for its own sake; change is resisted when it appears to threaten some of our deeper inner needs, such as the need for security or for control. Until we understand that people resist change because they feel a legitimate inner threat rather than simply because of rigidness and stubbornness, we will remain unable to manage their resistance to change.

This is why merely talking about the need to change and setting up programs is not sufficient to create fundamental change. However well intentioned the programs may be, they are likely to meet with considerable resistance or even failure if they do not take the critically important inner needs of the person into account.

The blocks to personal change, therefore, are on the inside, rather than on the outside. To implement effective change, we first need to understand the human being in much more depth. We must learn to listen to what is really important for others and to their deep motivations. As this happens, people will feel more free and willing to change. Our goal then must be to help individuals free themselves from fear. This inner freedom is the source of true flexibility and creativity.

The Way of the Creative Manager

Throughout history, creative managers have seen that new ways have been required. Today, the new way is an inner way. Moreover, because it is a personal way, it is a way that is open to millions of people.

The mark of creative managers is not a different way of doing but rather a different way of being. They appreciate that to manage the world around them, they must also manage the world within themselves. They must learn how to manage their inner processes.

This way of being is about understanding our own inner worlds better. It involves becoming clear about our motivations and how we can satisfy them; recognizing when we are angry and having constructive ways of expressing anger; learning to listen, both to others and to ourselves; seeing when we are stuck in old ways of looking at things; and learning how to think afresh. It is about understanding the creative process and knowing how to release it in our lives. It is about a new attitude to life.

Because this way is new to our culture, it is easily misunderstood. Sometimes it is dismissed as withdrawing from the world, a refusal to face practical issues. In reality, this way of being gets to the heart of the matter: an archer would never be criticized for pulling back his arrow on the bow.

Even when the value of this way of being is apparent, the way may be rejected as too difficult. Following this way is certainly not easy. This is not because the way itself is difficult, but because it is new. To tread this path means standing up for what is true and challenging past perceptions and beliefs. This requires vigilance, perseverance, and, above all, courage.

When we do embark upon this way, we may soon become discouraged and give up as we realize that we are hunting in the dark. Because this way is new, we do not yet have many of the inner skills we need to follow it. We must seek them out, rather than continuing to look for the key only where there is light.

The addition of inner ways of being to our outer ways can be considered as a marriage of contrasting values: To action, we bring allowing. To doing, we add being. To the alert mind, we bring a caring heart. To our knowing, we add the mystery of the unknown. To the desire for order, we bring an acceptance of uncertainty. To technology, we add people. And to the flights of our ideas, we bring the ground of the Earth. By bringing opposite values together within ourselves, we can confront the imbalance in our societies and in our personal lives.

Creativity is not just a matter of techniques and skills. Of course, techniques are helpful, but as many of us know, even when we use techniques for creativity, something is still missing. The process of creativity has an underlying mystery about it. What takes place is still beyond our control and beyond our awareness. It is as though the creative process has a life of its own that is always beyond our grasp. Techniques may take us to the door of this mystery; a new level of self-understanding is needed to enter more fully into the creative process. We need to learn how to engage and work with this hidden inner dimension.

The rest of this book is about beginning to understand how we can enter this mysterious process, seeing how it affects every facet of our lives, and learning how to use it. It is about deepening our understanding of who we really are and how we live, for the way of the creative process is the way of life.

3
The Creative Process

The concept of creativeness and the concept of the healthy, self-actualizing, fully human person seem to be coming closer and closer together, and may perhaps turn out to be the same thing.

—Abraham Maslow (1976)

We tend to think of creativity as the province of a chosen few individuals who have been flashes of brilliance and have left an enduring mark on humanity. We enshrine as our "gods of creativity" the thinkers Socrates, Plato, Aristotle, Buddha, Aquinas, Descartes, Russell, Wittgenstein, and Bateson; the artists da Vinci, Michelangelo, van Gogh, Renoir, Picasso, and Hockney; the writers Shakespeare, Milton, and Keats; the musicians Bach, Beethoven, Mozart, Tchaikovsky, and Stockhausen; the theorists Pythagoras, Newton, Copernicus, Maxwell, Einstein, and Hawking; the inventors Archimedes, Gutenberg, Watt, Babbage, Edison, Daimler, and Buckminster Fuller; and a thousand other celebrated individuals.

In focusing on such people as creative, however, we imply that those of us who have not left great marks on history are not creative or just occasionally and mildly creative. In truth, while we may not be like da Vinci or Einstein, we are all creative all of the time. Some of us have used our creativity in ways that have left a visible mark, while others have not.

To create means "to bring into existence." In this respect, each sentence we speak is a creative act, a choice to bring a thought into a form that can be communicated. It does not matter that a thousand people may have independently come up with the same or similar words at other times; our act is still

Note: From *The Farther Reaches of Human Nature* by Abraham Maslow. New York: Viking Press, 1976. Reprinted with permission of the publisher.

one of creation. As you read these words, you are exercising creativity; you are bringing images and ideas into existence in your mind. You express creativity in every decision you make, whether it be in resolving a conflict, organizing a presentation, or preparing a meal. Whatever you do, you are causing the world to change, you are bringing new forms into existence. Every thought and every action you ever make is an expression of creativity. To be alive is to create.

Valuing Our Creativity

Most of us do not normally regard all our thoughts and actions as creative. We feel that "real" creativity must bring into existence ideas and forms that are unexpected, that are new in the sense that no one else has created them, and that have lasting impact on the world. But would a person who thought up the theory of relativity without any knowledge of Einstein's work be any less creative than Einstein? Would Einstein himself have been less creative if no one had taken him seriously? Certainly, some of our creative expressions are new to the world, and a few may leave a lasting mark, but in terms of the inner processes of the mind, they are no more "creative" than any other of our creations.

If we judge creativity only by its external attributes—its originality and impact—we do ourselves a disservice. We do not see that creativity is, in essence, an internal process that is going on within us all, all of the time.

Once we get caught in the belief that we are not very creative, we are liable to fall into a self-confirming attitude. We may fail to see and appreciate our own creativeness and may unconsciously block its natural flow, proving to ourselves that we are not very creative. We may have ideas, but, believing that we are not very creative, we may ignore our ideas because they are ours. Ralph Waldo Emerson described this problem remarkably succinctly in his essay *Self-Reliance*:

> To believe your own thought, to believe that what is true for you in your own private heart is true for all men—that is

genius. Speak your latent conviction, and it shall be universal sense. We should learn to detect and watch that gleam of light which flashes across our own minds. Yet we dismiss without notice our own thoughts; they come back to us with a certain alienated majesty. Tomorrow a stranger will say with masterly good sense precisely what we have thought and felt all the time, and we shall be forced to take with shame our own opinion from another.

How often have we found another person taking all the credit for an idea that we had long ago? The other person is called "creative," while our own ideas remain ignored. More often than not, we undervalue our own thoughts, keep them to ourselves, and do not act on them.

However, as we shall see shortly, the creative process involves more than just having a new idea; it is also about turning that idea into form. Thomas Edison is revered as the inventor of the light bulb. But he did far more than just have a bright idea; it took him years of experimentation and hundreds of failures to succeed in producing a bulb that worked. Those people who trust their ideas, see the value in them, and follow them through are those who express their creativity—and thus are those we regard as "creative." Unexpressed creativity is not the creativity we seek.

In those areas in which we do express our creativity, we may often find it flowing along well-worn channels. A person may be a good cook, but not see himself as creative in other arts. Another may have many creative ideas in computer programming, but become blocked when she must manage a team. Another person may express his creativity in graphic design but not in solving problems. In those areas in which our creativity flows easily and freely, we accept our gifts, often hardly noticing them. Yet we notice those areas in which we are blocked and dismiss ourselves as not creative. We again make creativity something special, beyond us, out of reach.

Like many other human attributes, our creativity can, in its early stages, be fragile and vulnerable. As children, most of us were brimming with creativity; we invented new games, composed new sentences, created new worlds in our imagination, made castles from scraps of wood, and developed friendships. Then we went to school, perhaps anticipating that learning, too, could be part of this creative play. Yet all too often, we gradually lost the art of play. As we grew up, learning became more serious. Our creative potential often fell dormant, was sometimes denied, and for most of us, was channeled in a few approved directions. No wonder many of us finished school feeling some inner lack and disappointment. Free-flowing creativity became like a lost dream, a dim remembrance from the past now replaced by a highly developed aptitude for rational thinking.

A logical mind and a critical faculty are certainly assets, especially when it comes to solving complex problems. However, the creative process also draws upon the nonrational, unseen, mysterious aspects of the mind. An overreliance on rational modes of thought can be a further block to our natural creativity. At its worst, our addiction to rationality can lead to a cynicism that denies any creativity whatsoever in us.

Creativity is encouraged by an openness of thinking, a willingness to live for a while with conflicting ideas and not have the solution come immediately, an inquisitiveness that looks for information and an eagerness to learn, an appreciation of the workings of the unconscious and a preparedness to play with the imagination, and a readiness to stand back and question assumptions and beliefs.

We often think of creativity as having a bright idea, a flash of insight, an "aha!" But it involves far more than that. It usually takes a lot of thinking, conscious and unconscious, before the inspiration can emerge. Einstein pondered on some inexplicable experimental results for many years before coming upon the Special Theory of Relativity. Nor is coming up with a new idea the end of the creative process. The new idea must be expressed and given form, and this too can take a lot of time and work.

Those whom we revere as "creative" are, more often than not, people who recognize that there is a process at work in creativity and who are willing to work with this natural process. Often, the rest of us unwittingly get in its way.

Becoming Aware of the Creative Process

To see the creative process in action, let us look at some brain-teasers of the kind often given as a test of "creative problem solving." As well as trying to solve the problems, be aware of the process of solving them, the stages that you are going through. (If you know the solutions to all of the problems, see if you can recall the process you went through when you first solved them.)

> *Problem One.* You are asked to divide a cake into eight equal pieces, but you are only allowed to make three cuts in the cake. How do you do it?

Try to solve the problem before reading on.

You probably noticed yourself picturing the cake or even drawing it to get a quick feel for the problem.

Some of you may have seen a solution right away. If you could not see a solution, you may have experimented with some cuts, perhaps imagining dividing the cake into four equal pieces with two cuts.

Then you probably became stuck. You may have gone back and tried some different cuts, or you may have just looked at your drawing or imagined your cake with two cuts and wondered how one more cut could get you four more pieces.

The longer you remained stuck, the more likely you were to become frustrated. You may even have given up and decided to read on.

Then suddenly, out of the blue, you may have seen a solution. You let go of an assumption that you had made about the problem, which allowed you to see another way of tackling it.

Finally, just to make sure that you had indeed found a solution, you probably counted up the number of pieces and checked quickly that they would all be the same size.

For those readers who are still stuck, one of the assumptions that you may have is that the cake is not three dimensional. Seeing through this assumption may lead you to a solution. Another assumption you may hold is that the pieces of the cake

Figure 3.1. Creativity Problem Two.

cannot be moved around. Seeing through this assumption can lead to another solution.

> *Problem Two.* Look at Figure 3.1. You are asked to draw four straight lines through the nine dots, without lifting your pen or pencil off the paper, so that all nine dots are linked; that is, every dot has at least one line passing through it.

Although the problem shown in Figure 3.1 has been around for years, it still illustrates the creative process well. Some of you may know the answer to this problem. If so, try to find a solution using just three straight lines—again, do not lift your pen off the paper.

Once more, notice the process that goes on inside your head as you try to solve the problem. You make an initial assessment of the problem and try some solutions. When these fail to satisfy the requirements, you may do some rethinking and experiment with other possible solutions. Perhaps you become stuck and feel frustrated and you may say to yourself, "Well, this proves that I am not very creative."

As in the first problem, your frustration is probably the result of being stuck within a set of assumptions, a way of seeing the problem. Most people, on initially approching this problem, "see" the nine dots as defining a square and unconsciously assume that the sides of the square present a boundary beyond which the lines cannot go. But this restriction is not stated in the instructions. Try again to solve the problem by experimenting with lines that end outside the square.

Those people who have solved the problem using four lines but remain frustrated by a three-line solution are almost certainly being held up by a different assumption. If you are a good logical thinker with a little mathematical training, you can even "prove" that it is impossible to link all nine dots using only three lines. Proving that it cannot be done certainly may ease your feeling of frustration but only proves its impossibility within a certain way of viewing the problem. You are probably viewing the dots as points and thus trying to solve the problem with lines that go through the center of each dot—but no one said they had to.

Those people who want to give up on the problem are encouraged to do so. Read on, and see if the answer suddenly comes to mind later.

Phases in the Creative Process

The phases that you went through in trying to solve the previous two problems are fundamental to the creative process. Whenever we want to solve a problem, discuss another way of doing something, compose a report, build a new team, develop a strategic plan, discuss personal development issues, plan a vacation, or redecorate the house, we follow a similar pattern. Even as you read these pages and learn new ways of thinking and acting, the process is operating. Of the various ways of charting the creative process, the model that we shall focus on here has five phases: preparation, frustration, incubation, insight, and working out.

- Preparation involves analyzing the task, gathering data, looking for patterns, trying out ideas, and questioning assumptions.
- Frustration occurs when we are unable to resolve the issue; feel bored, irritated, or despondent; and doubt our own ability.
- Incubation occurs when we give up trying, put the issue on hold, and hand it over to the unconscious mind.

- Insight is the inspiration, the "aha," the moment we normally associate with creativity.
- Working out involves testing our insights and giving them form.

The phases may not always occur as such discrete stages or in the same order. Sometimes they may occur so quickly that we hardly notice them. At other times, the phases may occupy us for hours, days, or even years. Nor are the boundaries between the different phases necessarily clear cut.

It is important to see creativity as a process such as this; if we only see it as the moment of insight, we are likely to undervalue the other equally important, although less striking, aspects of the process. On the other hand, if most of our education and training has led us to focus on gathering information and making analyses, we may again see only part of the process. We will tend to jump to the final phase before giving the less conscious aspects of the process time to mature. If we are to allow creativity to flow more freely in all aspects of our life, we first need to become more aware of the characteristics of each phase of the creative process and understand how to work with the process as a whole.

Preparation
Starting on the Way

Thomas Edison said that genius is 1 percent inspiration and 99 percent perspiration. Great authors sometimes spend years researching their subjects. Some artists are renowned for the many detailed preliminary sketches they make before embarking upon a painting. Scientists may spend years designing and building a crucial experiment.

Yet most of us, in our everyday creativity, frequently wish that the creative process did not involve such hard work. How often, when starting to write a report, design a new program, or plan a strategy, have we felt daunted by the task ahead? We know that it is going to entail a lot of hard work, and what we would really like is to be able to bypass the "perspiration" and get our ideas out quickly and effortlessly.

We know in our heart, however, that whenever we have produced a work that we have cherished the quality has come from the time and energy we put into the task, not just from the novelty of the insight. We also know that we can derive much joy and fulfillment from this preparation phase.

This phase has many different activities connected with it. When faced with a problem or a project, we first try to get a feel for the issue at hand and decide on our objectives. We may need to address several questions: What parameters apply? Who else needs to be involved? Are there time constraints or financial considerations that we need to be aware of?

Gathering Information

An early task in this phase is gathering together all the information that we need, which brings to light everything we know about the issue. If it is a project we have had an interest in for some time, we will have a lot of information about the project filed away in the back of our mind, some of it probably quite hazy. The more we think about the problem, the more we can pull this knowledge into the foreground. People often report that they are surprised at just how much they already know about an issue when they mass all of the information together.

We can also gather data from other sources: reports, articles, and books; people who have some experience in the field; or people who are closely involved in the issue at hand. A major decision may involve lengthy research, with a team of people working on the task. As time consuming and energy consuming as this research can be, it usually pays off.

Do not be afraid to seek advice at this stage. In one corporation with which we were working, the director of a design team had to present a detailed proposal for the energy plant of a new industrial installation in twelve weeks. The deadline was inflexible, and looking at all the research he had to do, the director "proved" that he could not complete the project on time. He saw himself as facing an impossible task. When we questioned him, he admitted that people in other divisions of his company had already gathered much of the information he needed. Asked why he did not approach them for assistance, he replied that they would resent his taking up their time on this issue and would not be willing to give him help in the future when he really needed it. What he had not allowed himself to see was that now was a time when he really did need their help.

It is easy for us to judge this manager as being weak, nonassertive, or incompetent and to find ourselves thinking, I would not have blocked myself like he did. But beware, many times the things that hold us back in the creative process are the apparently silly personal issues.

As we gather more and more information about a problem, our understanding of the central issue deepens; we begin to uncover the core of the problem and see more clearly the heart of the matter. This deepening understanding can often lead us to see the issue in another light. Sometimes, we may need to redefine a problem several times. Each redefinition can bring us closer to the essence of the issue. In redefining an issue, we may find that the real problem is very different from the one we have set out to solve. The importance of being clear on what the real issue is hardly needs emphasizing—the last thing we want to do is come up with a creative solution only to find out later that we have solved the wrong problem.

Another part of the preparation phase is to explore trial solutions. The problem may be similar to others we have solved in the past. Perhaps the experience we gained from solving them can help us in our search for a solution. Or other possible approaches may spontaneously come to mind. At this stage, any possibility is certainly worth exploring; however, we should not forget that these are only trial solutions. Only occasionally will a trial solution lead us directly to a solution for the whole problem, in which case we can move on to the working-out phase. Usually, the period of exploring trial solutions is an important part of expanding our awareness of the problem.

One aspect of preparation that is commonly overlooked is the need to become aware of and challenge the basic assumptions that we bring to the task. We are unconsciously conditioned by our past thinking and experience. Our minds tend to get stuck in fixed tracks that limit the way we approach the task and the sort of solutions that we look for. An open mind is crucial to the creative process, so much so that Chapter Five will be devoted to questioning our assumptions.

Taking Time for Preparation

In some respects, we are always preparing to solve new problems. We are continually taking in new ideas, facts, and experiences, any of which could be data for a future problem. This is why "creative" people are frequently those who are always taking in new information, whether through reading, listening to lectures, watching documentaries, or some other way. This information may not be directly relevant to their current work, but by expanding their general knowledge, they are preparing themselves in a general way for problems to come.

The deliberate preparation that occurs when we settle down to solve a problem is a time to work hard with the conscious mind, a time to be unafraid of cool, critical analysis and mental clarity and rigor. This is not usually a great problem for the person who has been taught that these mental qualities are important. Most managers have been trained to seek clear and concise definitions of a problem and to set objectives. They know how to gather data and how to analyze it and are very good at drawing upon past experience.

However, many of us have difficulties in the preparation phase because of our impatience. In our eagerness to get through the phase, we often do not give ourselves time to explore the issue to the depth it requires. Instead, we tend to seize upon possible solutions and go for premature closure. Although this phase may be only one of five phases in the creative process, experience has repeatedly shown that, in general, the more time that is given to it, the better the quality of the final solution.

When deciding how long to spend on preparation, we tend to be torn between two contradictory choices. On the one hand, we find it hard to accept that however long we spend on preparation we will never have all the information we need. It would be more comforting if we knew that we had thought through every eventuality, explored every avenue, and foreseen those surprises that are so obvious in retrospect.

On the other hand, we tend to want to get the problem out of the way. Almost invariably, this urge takes priority over the need for a thorough analysis. Thus, in most organizational settings, we spend far too little time in preparation.

This almost universal tendency to move on to the insight and working-out phases as quickly as possible is very apparent in our seminars on creative management and problem solving. Our approach is to encourage participants to spend a lot of time focusing on the preparation phase, often as much as three-quarters of the total time of our work together. At first, people find this emphasis difficult to accept; they feel they are wasting time rather than getting on with the real job of finding a solution. But this "wasted time" is crucial. Not only are people gaining much deeper insights into the nature of the problem during this time, but they are also allowing for the appearance of more appropriate solutions. The attitude we try to instill during our seminars is one of creative restraint. The creative manager holds off going for solutions as long as possible—and then holds off a little longer, even though this delay may be frustrating.

Frustration
Hints of the Mystery

The solution to a problem can, as we have mentioned, sometimes come during the preparation phase. An obvious solution may indeed work, past experience may contain the answer, or suddenly, as if out of nowhere, we may have a flash of inspiration. Occasionally, the problem may not be solved but rather "dissolved" as we realize that there is not really any problem after all. At other times, however, after we have done a lot of data gathering, thinking, and analysis and have explored all possible solutions that have presented themselves, the problem is still there and still needs to be resolved. In short, we are "stuck."

At this point, we enter the frustration phase of the creative process. For example, an artist may find himself becoming frustrated when he just cannot get a face to express the feelings he wants it to, despite having tried again and again. A scientist may feel frustrated that she cannot get the solution to a set of equations, although she knows a solution must exist and she has all the skills she needs to find it. A person writing a paper or a report may become frustrated as he begins to realize that it is not coming out right, that it is not expressing what he really wants to say. People in a meeting may feel frustrated as time moves on and the group does not reach a decision.

Traditional descriptions of creativity have tended to omit frustration from the process. Not being able to come up with a solution seems to be the opposite of creative thinking. In addition, the feeling of being stuck can feel like a barrier to our creativity. From this point of view, the sooner that we get out of frustration the better.

Another very strong reason that we avoid frustration is because it is, by its very nature, uncomfortable. We may feel tense, irritated, angry, discouraged, inadequate, lost, bored, or very often simply tired. We may imagine that we "should" have the answer by now and may begin to doubt that we will ever come to a satisfactory solution. Or we may feel that even if a solution exists, we will never find it in time. We do not enjoy being frustrated and want to get out of it as quickly as possible—although, as we shall see shortly, this attitude may not always be the most useful way of dealing with frustration.

Frustration can also manifest itself as a sense of personal failure, a stong tendency to doubt our own abilities, and a feeling of inadequacy. We may say to ourselves: I'm not good enough. I've deluded myself; I am not up to this task. I should never have taken this project on; it's clearly too much for me. Someone else would have found an answer by now. This is the time when we are inclined to say to others, "I told you so. I am simply not a creative person."

Even when we remain confident in our abilities, we may still feel some temporary inadequacy. We think: I'm too tired and run down at the moment to be creative. I can't do this because I slept so badly last night. I've got a mental block about this subject. I am not in a creative mood these days.

Frustration Misperceived

Frustration is a much misunderstood phenomenon. It is seldom allowed for or encouraged in our educational system. Ability is seen as getting on with the task, getting things done, achieving and succeeding. Being stuck is regarded as a sign of poor ability. Instead of learning to recognize and handle frustration, students often see it as a barrier to success, a personal handicap.

The situation in the workplace is the same. A person struggling with a problem tends to be asked, "Haven't you done it yet?" "Why do you find it so difficult?" "Perhaps we should put someone else on the task?" The underlying implication is that struggling with a task and becoming frustrated is wrong; only striding smoothly and easily toward an answer is "right" and "good."

Because of this cultural conditioning, we see frustration as a sign of personal failure. We imagine that being blocked is the opposite of being creative. Yet were Michelangelo and Beethoven never blocked? Did Sartre, Wittgenstein, Russell, and Pope never find themselves stuck? Did Newton's ideas always flow smoothly and easily? Van Gogh described how frustration was a major part of his life. Einstein lived with it for years. Iaccoca at Chrysler felt at times that he was being thwarted at every turn.

Because we experience frustration in such a negative way, we assume that it is not part of the creative process. To many of us, realizing that it is a part of the process is a revelation. Frustration can be a signal that something is missing, that something else needs to be done. Perhaps there are aspects of the problem we have not explored; perhaps there are hidden assumptions that have led us in the wrong direction. Perhaps it is simply time to step back and sleep on the problem. From this perspective, frustration is a very important part of the process that should be explored rather than pushed out of the way.

At this point, it is important to distinguish between primary and secondary emotions. A *primary emotion* is a description of a person's existential reality. The feeling that we cannot solve a problem may in fact be valid. Perhaps we do not have the necessary skills or training, a crucial piece of information is missing, or we need help from people with strengths that we do not have. An advertising executive, for instance, may need help and guidance before she can resolve a difficult personnel issue in her department. Similarly, a good production manager would not necessarily be expected to be able to handle a complex strategic issue. In such cases, the feeling of "I can't" is a realistic assessment of how things are, of what we can do and what we cannot do. These are feelings to respect. They denote personal maturity in being able to acknowledge our own limitations. They may be a signal to develop our skills, seek more information, or get help from our friends.

Secondary emotions, on the other hand, are the real villains. They are based upon neurotic fears from the past and usually reflect an anxiety about our own self-worth. A feeling of "I can't" that arises from a secondary emotion may be nothing more than a put-down of ourselves, a habitual tendency not to trust our own abilities. This is the self-talk that says, "I'm not good enough. I've never been any good at this sort of thing." Such reactions are seldom valid and are certainly not helpful in the creative process. These are the feelings to step beyond.

To be able to separate these two types of emotion is important; it allows us to step back and listen to what the frustration is really telling us. It becomes a signal that can help us decide which way to move in our own creative process.

Managing Frustration

For most people, frustration is the most difficult phase of the creative process. Even those people who understand the role of frustration in the creative process may still react to it by pushing on regardless, hoping for a breakthrough, or by jumping to a snap solution. Often, only in retrospect can we see that we were in a classic period of frustration and that we should have stopped pushing for a solution an hour ago or even a week ago.

Unlike preparation, which is a deliberate, conscious process, frustration cannot be handled by using mental skills and techniques. Thus, it is often misunderstood and dismissed. During a period of frustration we really need to have trust and confidence in the creative process and in ourselves. But, in our desire to get past it, we stop ourselves from seeing frustration for what it is: a signal to stop—stop pushing, stop doing, and start listening.

This requires a very different attitude from that which most of us have learned and are used to. We tend to look for things to do that will relieve us of our difficulties; but any action we take will, more than likely, only make our frustration worse.

Frustration can feel like a mental wall that we are hitting against; it often seems that there is no way forward. However, once we recognize that the creative process as a whole is an interplay of inner and outer processes, frustration becomes less like a wall and more like a permeable membrane separating the inner from the outer. We must learn to pass through this membrane.

As long as we regard frustration as a sign of inadequacy, we may fear that others will see us as inadequate if we expose our feelings of discomfort and "failure." Acknowledging our feelings of frustration helps us put them in their proper perspective, as signals to be listened to rather than barriers to be resented. We thus shift from being a victim of our feelings to being able to choose how we deal with these feelings. Recognizing feelings as a message from within can help us to step back from the rational, analytical mode of thinking, stop trying to push ahead, and instead consider the questions: What is missing? What else do I need? Given that I am stuck, how should I proceed?

We should learn to accept these feelings of confusion and uncertainty as a natural part of life. For most of us, this acceptance usually does not come easily. We feel much more comfortable if we know where we are going and how long it is going to take us to get there. To wait, not knowing how long this discomfort will last, requires courage—particularly when everyone around us seems to be clamoring for a solution.

If we can hold this "creative tension," we may sometimes break through to another level of thinking, a new way of seeing the problem. Perhaps information that we have forgotten suddenly comes back. Sometimes a clue can come from unexpected questions or misgivings. Consider the following example reported to us from one of our clients:

> Bill and I were working on a lengthy report. We were well into the second draft when a feeling of unease gradually came over me. I began to wonder whether we had actually got things in the right order. This was disconcerting, for we'd spent considerable time organizing the material in the first place. The last thing I wanted to do was create a problem where none existed, particularly at this stage. I also knew that a major restructuring was the last thing that Bill would want to do. But I continued to feel troubled, so I told him what I was feeling.
>
> Fortunately his reaction was not exasperation. He took my question seriously and we began to look at what would happen if we changed the order. As we did we became increasingly aware that the key theme, the message which underpinned everything in the report, had not been given sufficient emphasis. The problem was not one of order, but content.

In this case, although the question itself may have been unwarranted, it did, nevertheless, have a basis. It was a sign that another message was trying to come through. Had they ignored or suppressed the question, chances are they would not have noticed the weakness in their report or perhaps would not have noticed it until the report was completed and submitted.

Thus, whenever seemingly awkward questions arise, honor them and give them space for consideration. Frequently, the question will be a disguised expression of a deeper discomfort or frustration that has not been fully expressed and does need attention. Acknowledging a nagging question, however irrelevant or foolish it may seem, can allow us to step back and open up to what lies behind it. What we find may be far from irrelevant or foolish.

The most important thing to do with frustration is to reinterpret it: to stop seeing it as something to get rid of and instead to allow ourselves to feel it. We need to value it as a difficult but essential phase in the creative process.

Allowing ourselves to feel frustration does not mean walking around endlessly doing nothing but rather recognizing the feeling as totally natural and learning to "read" it for what it means. The better we know ourselves as individuals, the better we know how to read the messages that our frustration is sending us. For a person whose staying power is slight and who tends to become frustrated quickly, the feeling can be a sign not to give up but to persevere. For someone whose tendency is to go on and on gathering data in order to defer making decisions, frustration may well be a sign to stop for the time being and go on to the next phase of the creative process: incubation.

Incubation
Allowing the Mystery

A newly laid egg will not hatch without a period of incubation, during which the chick can develop to the stage where it is ready to break out of the shell. So, too, ideas often need to be "incubated" before they can "hatch." And, as with the development of the chick, this process happens out of sight; it is a development that takes place beneath our conscious mind. During incubation, nothing seems to be happening; all we do is keep the ideas warm.

Incubation is a time to rest ourselves from conscious thinking about the task at hand, a time to leave the problem alone. It is a time for something completely different.

Sometimes, we may enter incubation deliberately, knowing that after "sleeping on the problem" we may well see things differently or come up with fresh ideas. More often, however, we find ourselves pushed into this phase. Having spent a lot of time in preparation, and probably some time in frustration, we may think, I can't go any further. I give up. When the frustration is particularly strong, we may think, I've had enough – to hell with it. Sometimes, the pressure of other duties and tasks may dictate that we leave the problem for now and come back to it later. Or we may simply be interrupted by people who need our attention for a while. Incubation can occur in brief interludes, such as during the time we go to get a cup of coffee, or over long periods, such as a vacation or a week of focusing on something else.

Like frustration, incubation is a part of the creative process that is not always given as much importance and value as it deserves. It is not something that we are taught to do at school or in management training. And our efficiency-oriented culture inclines us to see this stepping back and doing something different as a waste of time. Yet much can happen while our conscious mind is not thinking about the problem.

Many creative people know that the quality of their solutions is greatly improved by handing the issue over to the unconscious for a while. The novelist Graham Greene, for example, deliberately gave time to this phase. Having completed all his conscious research and gathered all the facts, experiences, and impressions he needed, he would not immediately sit down and start writing. Instead he would wait, letting his unconscious mind take over and watching what it had to tell him in his dreams. Only when the dreams had gathered and settled would he begin to write.

A rather different approach is taken by Seymour Cray, founder of Cray Computers. For many years he has been dividing his time between building the fastest, most powerful computers in the world and digging a tunnel that starts beneath his house. "When I get stumped, and I'm not making progress, I quit. I go and work in the tunnel. It takes me an hour or so to dig four inches." For Cray, digging this tunnel is more than a simple diversion. Says the chairman of the company, "The real work happens when Seymour is in his tunnel."

Incubation can also be unintentional. We have all experienced times when we have taken our attention off a problem for a brief moment and an idea that has been stubbornly hiding from us suddenly pops up. A friend recounted the following incident:

> A colleague and I had spent the best part of a morning at a computer terminal working on the development of a new program. But the calculations involved were so complex that there seemed no way we could fit it all into the memory available. Every solution we tried eventually ran out of space. But we didn't want to give up; we both felt that it must be possible.

> In the end we decided to take a break and go across the street for a cup of coffee. We had walked down one flight of stairs and halfway across the street when suddenly the answer came. We solved it then and there. Over coffee we checked out the details and found we did indeed have a workable solution.
>
> Now I know that we could have sat at the terminal for another two hours and still not come up with this solution. But switching off for just half a minute was enough to give a new approach time to surface. In some way I must have known the solution all along, but without this stepping back it could not get through.

Stopping for a cup of tea or coffee is just one way we can allow incubation. Others include playing with the children or going for a meal or a walk. Some people talk to other people as a distraction, read newspapers, or watch old films on television. A great many people just go to sleep. Other people soothe themselves with a massage, take a bath, or meditate. But the most common, and perhaps least noticeable, form of incubation is simply getting on with something else that needs to be done.

Listening to Our Unconscious

The insights of the unconscious mind cannot always be put into words, which is one reason why our rational, analytical thinking prevents us from seeing them. When they do come through, they often appear as a feeling or an emotion. We may begin to become aware of misgivings we have about the route we are taking. We may notice a niggling feeling that more information or more analysis is needed. Or we may discover an underlying sense of acceptance about an issue that puts an earlier frustration into perspective.

Allowing deep feelings to surface in a period of incubation can be invaluable in resolving problems in our personal life. During periods of total frustration, the act of stepping back may bring about a turning point. For example, a marriage may be going through a rocky period. Having tried everything they can think of to resolve the crisis, the partners may sense the need to get away to somewhere quiet—in the countryside, by the sea, or in the mountains. In this unhurried environment, devoid of the usual pressures, they may receive, almost unbidden, new and clear perceptions of the relationship.

Sleep is one of the best incubators, for during sleep, the activity of the conscious, rational mind is at its lowest. Not only may we wake in the morning with new perspectives on a task but the unconscious may also speak to us in our dreams. Sometimes we may find ourselves dreaming about the problem, and our dreams may show us aspects of the situation we had not seen before.

Philip Goldberg, in *The Intuitive Edge*, vividly describes how the inventor Elias Howe dreamt about the key to completing a workable sewing machine.

> Howe had labored for several years and was one small detail away from his goal. Then one night he dreamed he has been captured by a tribe of savages whose leader had commanded him to finish his machine or else be executed. In the dream the terrified inventor was surrounded by warriors leading him to his death when he suddenly noticed that his antagonists' spears had eye-shaped holes near the points. Howe awakened from his dream and whittled a model of the needle with a hole near the point instead of in the middle of the shank [1983, p. 177].

Some people find it useful to keep a dream diary, particularly when they have a major problem to solve. Going back over our dreams can reveal inner responses and feelings that we never allow ourselves to see while we are awake and rational. We do not need to analyze our dreams deeply but simply look to see what we are trying to say to ourselves. In this respect, we can unravel our dreams better than anyone else can. We have created the dreams; they are our symbolism, our interpretation. We have the key to understanding them.

Giving Time for Incubation

Being open to incubation is not always as easy as it might sound. We are so trained to think with our conscious minds and so consumed by the idea of getting to our goal in the shortest possible time that most of us find it very difficult to stop thinking about a problem. Moreover, the more frustrated we are, the harder it can be to stop worrying about finding a solution.

When we are under pressure, we may feel that we cannot possibly afford to take time off. Every minute seems precious. Yet, if the task is not going as smoothly or as quickly as we would like, the chances are that something else we know inside is not getting through to us. At these times, we cannot afford *not* to step back for a few minutes.

Other people's demands for an immediate decision also can make it difficult for us to take time. We have all received telephone calls in which someone asks us to make a decision on some issue. Seldom do we take time to mull over the decision; instead, we fall into the trap of believing that we must give an answer immediately. But how often have we later wished that we had waited for a while before replying? The truth is, we rarely have to answer a question right away just because someone asks us to do so. We can usually wait twenty-four hours before we answer. If the decision must be made more quickly, we can usually wait ten minutes, take a quick stroll, or have a cup of tea while we see what our inner feelings are saying. It is surprising how often new perspectives can come to us in just a few minutes on our own, away from the pressure of someone's standing over us or waiting on the other end of the telephone line.

Even when we know that a period of incubation may be just what we need, we still have to contend with others who may view our taking time off as a sign of laziness. Taking time for incubation can be particularly difficult in a company that sends the message, "We pay you to work, not dream." Some organizations, however, are recognizing the value of giving people time to step back. A British television company, for instance, pays one of its gifted young documentary makers to go away alone to a small country inn for a couple of days to clarify his ideas before starting his "official" work on a film. The small cost of a bed and meals for two nights is repaid richly in the imaginative depth of the ideas that come to this person during these solitary days of walking in quiet fields.

Taking time for incubation is as valuable and essential as taking time for preparation. Indeed, incubation could be considered to be another aspect of preparation. Preparation, as it is usually defined, involves conscious, rational analysis. Even when this phase is complete, we may still need to glean some vital information from our feelings and our intuitions.

Incubation can be thought of as a period of inner preparation. If we skip this phase, we miss out on a fundamental part of creativity. For creativity is something that springs from the unconscious mind far more than it does from the conscious mind. Our true potential is not just what we know in the sense of what is conscious; it is also what we "know" inside. It is this "inner knowing" that we most need to tap because both the mystery and the depths of our creativity reside in our unconscious mind.

A period of incubation can lead us in several different directions. We may realize that we need to gather more data, go back and analyze the situation in more depth, or return to some other aspect of the preparation stage. At other times, we may become frustrated again as the need to resolve the problem makes itself felt. Often, we find new ideas jumping into our mind, leading to possible solutions. When this happens, we have moved into a new phase of the process: insight.

Insight
Solving in Mystery

The essence of creativity is the birth of something new. Ideas that were previously unrelated suddenly come together, and from their new relationship a new idea is born. We have a flash of insight. Suddenly we see things in new ways, and new possibilities open up before us.

This is the phase of the creative process that we most readily associate with creativity and the phase that we are most attracted to. However, if we only see creativity as this moment of inspiration, then we remain helpless; we cannot do anything to make an insight occur—it seems to drop "out of the blue." If all we do is wait for inspiration, we are powerless victims of the process, and the chances are that nothing will happen.

The creative person recognizes that although insight appears to come from nowhere, it actually occurs as a result of everything that has gone before. The preparation, the mulling over of the problem, the analysis of data, the soaking of the mind in the issue, the frustration and its signals to look deeper or explore inner feelings, and the unconscious processes that happen during incubation all contribute toward creating a mental field in which the seed of insight can sprout.

Sometimes an insight may occur during the preparation stage; just thinking about the problem may be enough to trigger a new idea. Very occasionally, insights may occur in the midst of frustration, but usually our state of mind in this phase precludes such breakthroughs. Most often, we receive insights after or in the midst of a period of incubation. If people are asked where or when they have their best ideas, most respond with situations such as in the bath or shower, in bed, at the point of falling asleep or on waking in the morning, walking the dog, having a drink with a friend, or after making love, playing golf, or running. What is common to all of these situations is that they are not "work" situations. We are usually doing something quite unconnected with the problem and are in a relaxed state of mind.

A new idea may be triggered by something totally unconnected to the problem. A senior information system's manager related this story.

> It really came out of the blue! I was walking past the Natural History Museum when the word *Savannah* came. The word soon became a very vivid image. The meaning of the image then clearly developed. It all happened in a few seconds.
>
> I remembered how, when I was twelve years old, my father and I visited one of the first nuclear-powered ships. On a deck below, the guide opened a hatch and through a plexiglass floor we looked down into the engine

room. Down there was the mysterious, forceful, propulsive engine.

Now, twenty-four years later, this memory of the ship *Savannah* spoke to me and triggered a new realization: I don't have to know all about myself to go forward. The captain of the *Savannah* doesn't know and understand all about the atomic reaction inside his ship. But still, he can navigate it on a foggy night in unknown waters.

In situations like this, the disconnected idea acts like a seed, combining with an aspect of the issue at hand to create a new synthesis. And it is this synthesis that gives birth to a new insight.

Insight and Imagery

In many cases, insights come to us as images rather than words. When Einstein hit upon the key to the nature of light, he was not sitting at his desk solving differential equations. He was lying on a grassy hillside, looking up at the sun through half-closed eyelids, and imagining himself to be a light beam traveling from the sun to his eye. His inspiration occurred as an image, and it occurred after years of mental preparation and a lot of incubation.

The chemist Auguste Kekulé, who discovered the molecular structure of benzene, had a similar experience. At the time of his discovery, all known chemical structures were composed of linear chains of atoms. Like other chemists, he had tried in vain to fit the six carbon atoms and six hydrogen atoms of benzene into a chain that satisfied the rules of chemistry. One night, after a good meal and a couple of glasses of brandy, he settled down to relax by an open fire. Half-asleep, he watched the flames twisting and curling upon themselves, and in his mind, they seemed like snakes circling around to bite their own tails. He woke up with a start. Flames do not go around in circles, but carbon atoms in the benzene molecule could. Benzene, he suddenly realized, is a closed chain, a ring structure.

In a way, Kekulé already "knew" the answer. But his belief

that the structure must be in the form of a chain was blocking him. Only when he took his mind completely off the task could his unconscious speak to him and show him what it knew—and it spoke in the language of the unconscious, in images.

Insights are not always solutions in the accepted sense of the word. For example, a bright and enterprising sales manager had been given the task of launching a new product division in an area in which the company was weak and needed to catch up with its competitors. A few months before the launch of the division, he had a bewildering experience. He imagined the division as an eagle, which certainly seemed to fit his feeling that it was strong, powerful, and a potential leader. But when asked to imagine going inside the eagle, he was puzzled to find it hollow and empty.

Gradually his own inner knowing began to emerge. He realized that his project was missing something fundamental: senior management commitment. They were giving it lip service but not the full financial and strategic commitment it warranted. It was clear to him that the division would fail without their support. He approached the board members and told them what he really needed if the division was to succeed, but they could not hear him. After several attempts to reach them, he decided to leave and join another company. His insight had not so much solved his problem as resolved it. Had he not trusted his image and explored what his unconscious was trying to tell him, he would probably have battled on and met with failure. In fact, the new product division never did get off the ground.

Because insight is the phase of creativity that most people want to facilitate, many techniques such as brainstorming, lateral thinking, and synectics have been developed. While these techniques certainly can stimulate new ideas, they should not be seen as solutions to the problem of creativity. Their effectiveness is dependent upon the amount of groundwork and preparation that has gone before and the willingness of participants to move beyond the surface level of thinking. Used as part of the creative process, they can be very valuable (as we shall see later); but used as "solutions" to the "problem" of developing creativity, they can be deceptive.

Self-Trust

Insight is the magic of creativity. It is totally mysterious, never visible, and always beyond our grasp. We cannot bring ourselves to insight, and yet it happens; it comes to us. We say, "It occurred *to* me." In a moment of inspiration, something "breathes into" us. Our task is not to create an insight, but to be open to it and see it when it comes.

The key is a receptive state of mind. We may not be able to hunt down insights or choose the moment of an inspiration, but we do have a choice over how we receive inspirations when they come to us. We can either keep our mind open, welcoming the new ideas as they occur, or keep it firmly closed, preventing ourselves from seeing what our unconscious is offering us.

Thus, self-trust is an important personal quality in this phase. So-called creative people are not creative just because they have more ideas but also because they trust their ideas and are willing to explore them. Other people tend to dismiss their insights. They think, Oh, that's just my idea. It can't be worth much.

Self-trust means trusting not just our conscious thinking processes but also our unconscious ones. With this trust, we are able to listen to our frustration and hear what it is saying. We can open ourselves to incubation, knowing that it is time to hand the problem over to our inner knowing, and value the images and insights that come into our conscious mind, seemingly from nowhere. Remember that Leonardo da Vinci's inspirations and Newton's insights came "out of the blue," but they trusted them enough to follow them through.

Working Out
The Way into Form

To have an insight is one thing; to turn it into form is quite another. Countless people may have marveled at the colors in a sunset, but it takes the dedication and skill of a Turner or a Monet to capture that vision on canvas in a way that communicates with others. Many of us may have had insights into the joy and beauty of life, but it may take many months of hard work before an insight can be conveyed in the words of a Blake, Wordsworth, Emerson, or Shakespeare. Other minds may have had glimpses into the nature of light, but it was Einstein who was prepared to follow his intimations through. Many people may have had dreams of a personal computer that matched the needs of the "user on the street," but it was Steve Jobs and Steve Wozniak, the founders of Apple Computer, who got down to the task of making it a reality.

The phase of "working out" – of working the insight out of the mind and into the world, where it may be perceived – is a key part of being creative. Without this phase, the creative process is incomplete. It is not the number of bright ideas that someone has that makes a person creative, but rather how many of these ideas are worked out from the realm of ideas into the world of action. This is the mark of truly creative managers: the willingness to explore their bright ideas.

Working out is a highly pragmatic phase of the creative process. It is here that we flesh out and clothe our insight, and develop concrete steps for converting it into reality.

Until an idea is given a form, our creativity remains unmanifest and unknown. Whether the project in question is as small a task as organizing a meeting or as large as building a factory or creating a new high-tech company, implementation remains as important a part of the creative process as any other. Creative managers must be able to communicate their insights and inspire others to want to put those insights into practice; otherwise these insights will remain no more than private bubbles, bits of untested theory that are no more than fantasies.

Yet all too often, the working-out phase is undervalued. We may conceive many new ideas each day but may bring few into the world because we do not pay attention to how they can be implemented. Often, we are so amazed by our insight that we forget that we must turn it into form before it can have value. Having had a bright idea, we tend to think that the creativity is finished; we overlook the fact that working the idea out is as important a part of the creative process as preparation or incubation.

As with preparation, this phase takes time. We must try

out the idea, get feedback, and make improvements based on this new data. In our culture, we are often admonished not to give up, but the admonishment is usually accompanied by a heavy moral overtone—as if persevering should be a burden, something that goes against our natural life processes. Persevering, however, can be part of an exciting creative process if every "failed" attempt is a source of more information that is useful for perfecting the next attempt, rather than a cause for discouragement.

Phases of Working Out

The working-out phase can be considered in two stages. First, we test our insight. Having trusted our own insight enough to want to follow it through, we must now ask: Will it work? Does it satisfy the original requirements? Is it really an answer to the question at hand? How will it look in practice? This testing can take seconds or it can take months of analysis, confirmation, and exploration of hidden implications.

Often at this stage, what seemed to be a brilliant idea fails the test. We may have to return to incubation, or more likely be thrust back into frustration. We may become aware of a need for more preparation, the need to go back and think more deeply about the task, gather more data, or become more clear on our objectives. Only because Edison was not discouraged by continual failure but was prepared to see each "failure" as new data and repeat the creative process time and time again did he eventually perfect a lightbulb that worked. Once again, we see that the creative process is not a linear sequence of events but rather a dynamic process, any phase of which can lead into any other and that we may dive back into many times before a problem is solved.

Even if our insight does seem practical, the creative process is far from over. We then move into the second part of working out: implementation. This phase can be brief—filling in an answer in a crossword puzzle may take only a second or two—or it can occupy us for a very long time. The implementation of a new management structure, for example, may carry through into many of our daily tasks as we deal with the unforeseen issues that arise in other areas, the personal concerns of those involved, and the subtle effects the changes may have on people's relationships, communication, and approach to work. If we are establishing a new marketing program, the implementation stage may continue for many months or even years as we ensure that our ideas are turned into practical results.

Our skills, training, experience, aptitudes, tools, and resources are of prime importance in implementation. A creative composer needs a good "ear," a knowledge of musical theory, the ability to write music, experience of which instruments and voices will give form to her inspiration, and good instruments at hand before she can manifest her idea. A creative photographer needs a good "eye," the right film, a good camera, knowledge of how to use the capabilities of his equipment, experience of what types of lighting work best, and an understanding of optics to take good pictures. And a creative manager needs communication skills, an understanding of human motivation, an appreciation of individual strengths and weaknesses, a willingness to handle her own feelings, experience of which approaches are most likely to succeed, training in specific skills, and abilities in leadership and empowerment before she can successfully implement a change.

The Creative Process in Miniature

The implementation stage is the creative process in miniature. Testing out the insight in practice gives us more information; if our idea does not work the first time, we have useful information on how to make it work the next time.

During preparation we focus on the problem. During implementation we focus on our insight for solving the problem. As we try to translate our idea into reality, we may again come up against frustration, we may again retire into incubation, and we may again have insights into how we can best implement our idea.

Moreover, within every one of these creative loops the creative process is again operating. We may, for example, be stuck on exactly how to implement a certain aspect of organizational change. Suddenly we come up with the idea of changing a particular person's responsibilities. Then we may dive back into the creative process again as we wonder how to communicate this idea to the person in a way that will not be perceived as threatening. A flash of insight may come to us in the night, and we may arrange to meet the person the next day to present the idea. Again, the creative process is not far away as we contemplate how to structure the meeting: What to say first? How to deal with the other person's concerns?

And even when we have answered these questions, our conversation will be a miniature, almost imperceptible creative process in itself, as we take ideas and express them in words and gestures, occasionally pause in preparation, perhaps experience momentary frustration and, just when we are not quite expecting it, finding the right phrase coming to mind.

In one way or another the creative process runs throughout our lives. Whatever we are doing we are never apart from it. It is something we are involved in day and night. Indeed, it is part of being alive.

The Dance of Inner and Outer

We can think of the creative process as a dance between conscious and unconscious realms of thought. Conscious, rational deliberation on its own will not give us new ideas, nor will any amount of incubation if the mind has not first been prepared. To solve a problem we need to take it into our conscious mind and then hand it over to our unconscious mental processes. The problem is solved by a creative insight that comes from within, and the inner idea is in turn converted into outer action.

Yet, because the unconscious mental processes are hidden from our awareness, we too easily overlook them and come to rely predominantly upon the more tangible conscious realms of thought. As members of a materially developed and highly educated culture, we know a lot about the brilliance and perception of the conscious mind. We have become very good at rational thinking, analysis, and planning, and we know how to work with ideas and manage our own conscious processes. But we have ignored the equally valuable unconscious processes. Because they are mysterious and intangible, we have not known how to make use of them and have left them on "automatic," hoping that they will work for us and come up with ideas. Sometimes this happens, but more often than not our dependence on the outer aspects of thinking leaves us stranded at the very time that we most need our inner help.

Left and Right Brain in Creativity

This dance between inner and outer is reflected in a dance between the two sides of the brain. Over the last few years, much research has focused on the extent to which the left and right sides of the human brain are specialized in different types of mental function. The left side of the brain appears to be particularly good at rational thinking, working with numbers, linguistic processing, control of speech and writing, analyzing the verbal input we hear and read, and thinking in words. The right side of the brain, on the other hand, appears to be better at synthesizing ideas and visual-spatial tasks, such as judging shape, seeing patterns, and drawing pictures.

Although some more recent findings suggest that not all the differences are as clear cut as some of the early researchers were led to believe (for example, some verbal processing may be carried out by the right brain) this distinction has nevertheless caught the attention of many people, particularly with regard to the subject of creativity.

Observing that both the ability to visualize images and the ability to synthesize ideas are associated more with the right brain than the left brain and that these processes are closely connected with the generation of new ideas, some people have suggested that the right brain is the seat of creativity. Right-brain processes may indeed play a more important role than left-brain processes in the formation of insights, but to conclude that creativity itself is a right-brain process is to make the mistake of seeing creativity as only a flash of insight rather than as a process of which insight is only a phase, albeit an essential one.

If we look at creativity as a process, we see that both sides of the brain play very important roles. Preparation, focusing as it does on analysis, data gathering, logical thinking, and understanding, uses the functions associated with the left side of the brain. During incubation, when no conscious processing of the issue is taking place, it is difficult to say which side of the brain is dominant; both sides are probably equally involved. Insight is, as already suggested, primarily associated with right-brain functions, and the working-out phase returns us to the logical, analytical, verbal modes of thought associated with the left side of the brain.

Thus, we can see the creative process as an alternation between the left and right modes of thinking, which to some extent reflects the move from the outer, conscious mind to the inner unconscious and back to the conscious mind. However, equating the right side of the brain with the unconscious mind, as some people have done, is a mistake. Both sides of the brain are open to our awareness, and undoubtedly, vast realms of both remain hidden.

In our society, however, we spend more time and effort focusing on the abilities connected with the left side of the brain than on those of the right. A traditional education deals with the three Rs—reading, 'riting, and 'rithmetic—each associated more with the left side of the brain. Art, music, poetry, dance, and other mental skills associated more with the right side are generally given a low priority.

This bias is reflected in our everyday conception of a "bright" person. When someone is said to have "a good mind," we usually infer that he or she is good at thinking rationally, understanding ideas, and communicating articulately. On the other hand, someone who is very good at painting or playing a musical instrument may not be thought of as "brainy," unless he or she is also good at left-brain thinking.

Although some modern approaches to education pay more attention to right-brain skills, many of today's managers were schooled in the traditional way, and thus they are more fluent and confident in left-brain skills than in those associated with the right side of the brain. This educational bias is another reason why many of us tend to focus on the type of thinking we know best—preparation and working out—and leave the insight to occur in its own "mysterious" ways. To be more deeply creative, we need to balance our left-brain skills with those of our right.

Learning from the Process as a Whole

Learning to work with the creative process is not about learning new techniques; it is about learning to trust the creativity that is already within us all. This is a simple idea, but the consequences of this shift in perception are immense. It means that we can see ourselves as our own greatest resource. We do not have to wait for someone to "put" something into us or write ourselves off as not belonging to "the creative few."

We each negotiate the various phases of the creative process in a way that reflects our own individuality. It is important for us to become aware of the ways we respond to the process and also to recognize and appreciate how differently others may respond.

At this point it is worth considering your own strengths and weaknesses in the creative process:

- In preparing to solve a problem, do you
  - spend enough time defining and redefining your problem?
  - go too quickly for a solution?
  - question your assumptions?
  - continue working when you should be taking a break?
- When you start to become frustrated, do you
  - step back and accept the discomfort?
  - listen to what is trying to come through?
  - talk to someone about your feelings?
  - push on, hoping you can break through?
  - take it out on others?
  - believe you are not up to the task?
  - give up?

- How easy is it for you to turn your mind away from a problem and think about something else for a while?
- Do you make time for incubation?
- In what situations do insights tend to come to you?
- Do you value your own insights or too easily dismiss them?
- Are you full of ideas but seldom carry them through?
- In the working-out phase, do you
  - really test your insights before putting them into practice?
  - plan and organize in detail?
  - monitor and get feedback?
- How easy is it for you to dive back into the creative process again, just when you thought you had solved a problem?
- Are you open to the mystery behind the creative process, or do you tend to look for security in the past and in techniques?

The more we come to understand ourselves and our own relationship to the creative process, the more we begin to realize that the process is something we are working with and learning from throughout our lives. The more we learn from it, the more that creativity can flow into our life.

4

Creating the World We See

> The real magic of discovery lies not in seeking new landscapes but in having new eyes.
>
> —*Marcel Proust (1899)*

An essential aspect of creativity is learning to see things with "new" eyes. We all too easily look through the lens of the past rather than be open to seeing things as they are. If we are to respond creatively to the radically different times we are entering, we must be willing to challenge our old ways of thinking and learn to see things afresh.

Valuable as our experience of the past may be, it colors our view of the present and the future. How often do we respond to a person in a certain way today because of something she said a year ago? How much is our appreciation of a film affected by what the critics say? How often do we assume that the future is going to be like the past?

We should not underestimate the strength of our past conditioning. Without our realizing it, the past haunts almost every aspect of our life. Nor should we underestimate how difficult it can be to step out of it. Breaking free of conditioning is one of the key issues that corporate leaders struggle with as they attempt to manage change. In the words of the quality control manager of a Scandinavian manufacturing company:

> How can we get the supervisors on the factory floor to change their ideas on quality? They simply don't seem to understand that we are no longer living in the past. I know they have the ability and the expertise to change the process and improve the quality if they wanted. The problem is in their minds.

This problem is not limited to the more developed countries. The group managing director of an African conglomerate told us:

> If we are to continue to be a major force in the 1990s, we will have to create a completely new management style and working culture in this group. I do not know if the power of the past will let us do so. It is people's attitudes that have to change; the rest will follow.

Even some of the leading-edge organizations appreciate how easy it is to get trapped in the past. The directors of a major Dutch software company, which has doubled its turnover every year for the past ten years, realized that in order to cope with the needs of the growing market and the demands of the industry, they needed to break out of the old way of looking at corporate structure. They found that the optimum size of each of their working groups was fifty. Now, whenever a group reaches this limit, they create a new division. As one of the senior directors remarked, "We have to continue to keep open to new ways of thinking and organizing ourselves, or we are dead."

Many of the leading management commentators of today go to the heart of this debate. Gareth Morgan, in *Riding the Waves of Change*, asks:

> How do you encourage people to let your organization become flexible, to face the issues, so that you can approach a competitive situation competitively? How do you do it? I think it is critical. . . .
>
> In the past, managerial competence went hand in hand with the possession of specific skills and abilities; it now seems to involve much more. Increasingly, it rests in the development of attitudes, values, and "mindsets" that allow managers to confront, understand, and deal with a wide range of forces within and outside their organizations [1988, p. 54].

How We See the World

Learning to step back and think freshly and flexibly is a key to being a creative manager. But it is more than just our thinking that is conditioned by the past; the whole of our perception is unconsciously determined by what has gone before. Appreciating the implications of this idea is new for our culture. Yet if we are to manage our future with the creativity it demands, we must understand the mechanism of perception so that we can release ourselves from the bonds of the past. To do so, let us first step back for a few moments and look at how we see.

We know that light comes in through the pupil of the eye and is focused onto the retina, which creates electrical pulses that are fed back to the brain. From this information we create an image of the world around us. But how does the mind create this image?

Consider Figure 4.1. What do you see?

Figure 4.1. What Do You See?

What is happening in your mind as you try to make sense of the picture? First notice that you are once again entering the creative process. The visual data is in front of you, and you are probably testing different possibilities. You may also be experiencing a little frustration! You may even have had an insight; you may see a snow scene, a map, a person, inkblots, or some other object, or perhaps you still see just black and white shapes.

What is going on in your mind as you reach for different possibilities? Either consciously or unconsciously, you are comparing the data in front of you with some previous experiences. You are hunting in your memory for a match. When something does seem to match, you combine the data with your past, creating an image that you "see" on the page.

As we can see in Figure 4.2, what we experience in our minds as we look at such a picture is in fact the normal process of perception greatly slowed down. Incoming data is neutral; meaning is added by the past experience already filed in our mind. When new data comes in, the brain tries to find a match with past experience. When it finds a good match, the mind "sees"; it makes sense of the data.

If you turn to Figure 4.6 at the end of this chapter, you will see another collection of black and white shapes. This time, however, it is easy to make a match with past experience, and the process of seeing occurs so rapidly that you do not even notice it. You appear to be simply seeing an image that is on the page, but

Figure 4.2. How the Mind Creates Images.

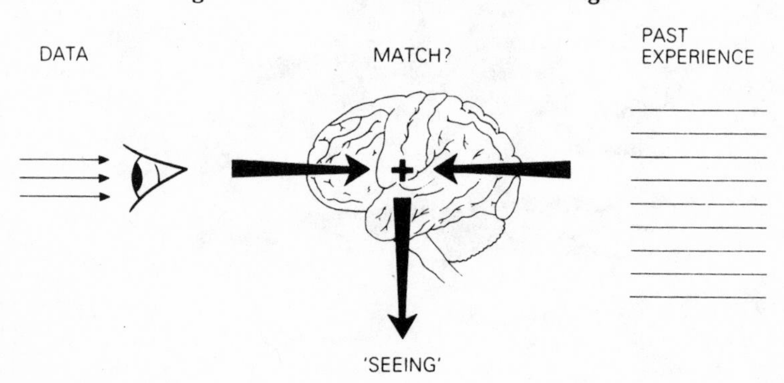

you have in fact created the picture of a cowboy out of the data on the page.

Return to Figure 4.1. What do you see now? You probably see the same image as in Figure 4.6. But the picture has not changed; you are seeing exactly the same data. However, now you have a past experience that matches easily with the data. The process of seeing is thus more automatic, faster, and obvious. It is the same creative process as before, but now much closer to normal speed.

Once we have made sense of the shapes, it is hard to let go of the image we have created. It is difficult to go back and see the shapes as a map, snow, inkblots, or whatever else you saw previously.

But where has the picture you now see come from? It may look as if it is on the page, but it is, in fact, inside your head. You have created it. The same happens with everything we "see"—apples, trees, cars, paper, people, computers—as well as everything we hear, smell, taste, and touch. The brain is continually matching the incoming flow of electrical pulses with past experiences and creating from this match an image in our mind of the world out there.

We create our world every moment of our life. This is creativity at its most pervasive level. And so powerful, constant, and ubiquitous is this creativity that we do not even realize it is happening.

This discussion may seem to be getting rather heady and a little removed from everyday creativity and management, but its implications are far reaching. They can relieve us from the domination of the past and free our creativity.

Mindsets

More than just our sensory perceptions are determined by the past. Once we have created a picture of the world, we add to this "reality" judgments, interpretations, and evaluations. And these, likewise, are based upon the past. We see a certain model of car and unconsciously judge its worth according to past reports and experiences. We may hear the words that someone says to us and unintentionally interpret them in a way that is based on our feelings for that person. We may be interviewing someone for a job and unknowingly evaluate him or her based on an accent and mannerisms.

These preconceptions we impose upon reality are known by psychologists as *mindsets*. Mark Brown, a consultant who has studied mindsets and their effects on our lives in considerable depth, defines them as "the psychological structures and schemas that make sense of our experience." In everyday speech, mindsets travel under many different names—attitudes, beliefs, biases, values, assumptions, prejudices, judgments, preconceptions, stereotypes. The following list presents some common examples of mindsets:

All politicians are corrupt.
People in business are only out to make money.
My mother still thinks of me as a child.
My children never listen to me.
Premarital sex is bad (or good).
Senior management is in control.
A good education will equip you for life.
Men with beards have something to hide.
It is difficult for women in business to get to the top.
My colleagues do not appreciate my real potential.
The early American settlers were hardy and adventurous.
People with Latin blood are warm hearted and emotional.
The harder I work, the more successful I will be.
English cooking is unimaginative.
Creativity cannot be taught.

People sometimes jump to the conclusion that to have mindsets is somehow wrong or unnecessary. In fact, mindsets are absolutely essential because without them we would not be able to understand and relate to the world in which we live. We would not be able to process and evaluate new experiences—we would be like a person trying to hang a hat on a wall without a hook. Mindsets are points of reference and anchors.

A mind without mindsets is structureless, amorphous,

and as useless as runny Jell-O. Imagine a manager trying to conduct an annual appraisal with a staff member without having any mindsets as to his or her performance, strengths, weaknesses, and potential for development. The manager would have no basis for making an intelligent evaluation.

Although mindsets are essential as current reference points, they are not absolute truth, only opinions. As such, they need to be regularly updated. Running an annual appraisal on the basis of last year's mindsets is clearly foolish. Yet how often do we unconsciously allow this to happen and thus remain trapped in the past?

We need to learn to step back and become aware of our own mindsets and appreciate how much they condition our experience of reality. For the creative manager, this action is often the first step in developing greater flexibility.

Seeing the World in Different Ways

If we hold on too tightly to one mindset, we do not allow other perspectives to come into our mind, although there are many ways of seeing the same data. Take, for example, the illustration shown in Figure 4.3.

Past experience leads us to see these twelve lines as a cube. But we can see this cube in two ways: as a cube seen from above or as one seen from below. Because we have been more used to seeing box-shaped objects from above than from below, most people find it easier to see the cube as though from above. But the other perspective is equally valid. With a bit of practice, we can change back and forth between the two perspectives without much effort.

We might ask, Which is it really—a cube from above or below? In fact, it is neither. All that the figure contains is twelve lines. We have created two different perceptions of this data. And, moreover, we have created a three-dimensional figure out of two-dimensional information.

Similarly with mindsets, the same data can often be interpreted in two radically different ways. For example, in an advertising campaign on British television, a national newspaper

Figure 4.3. A Cube from Above or from Below?

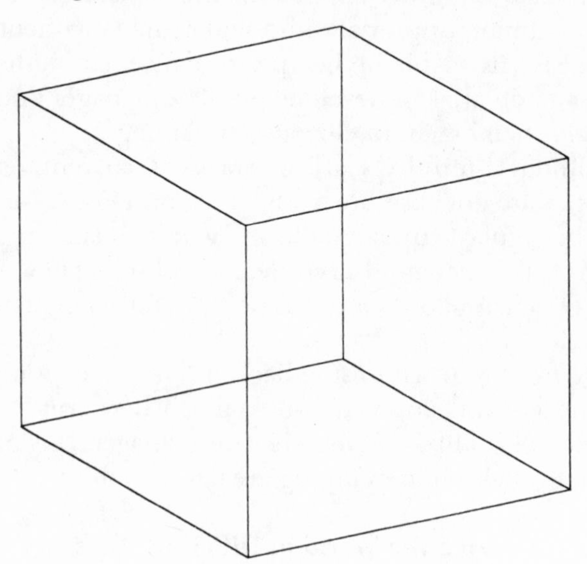

tried to put across the idea that, unlike other newspapers, it did consider alternative perspectives. The film showed a young "skinhead" jumping onto a businessman. It looked as though he was attacking the man. Then the camera pulled back to reveal a crane load of bricks that were about to fall on the businessman. The skinhead had pushed him out of the way just in time. The message is clear: it is foolish and dangerous to leap to habitual conclusions. It is important to step back and see if there are alternative views before reacting out of old mindsets.

We bring our own individual mindsets to every situation. For example, many Western men are more sexually attracted to slender women than to overweight women. Is this preference a matter of simple physical "chemistry" or is it the result of social conditioning, or in other words, the result of a group mindset?

In a particular Pacific island community, men find large, overweight women attractive and desirable, so much so that the headmen feed their women constantly and prevent them from exercising so that the women become enormously fat. In the West, such women would be hospitalized for gross obesity and their rolls of flab would be viewed with disgust. But on this island, under the potent influence of the social mindset, the men find these women to be sexually arousing.

Cultural mindsets also change with time. Plump Victorian gentlemen were considered desirably "well formed" in the 1870s. A hundred years later, trim athletic men were "in," and being plump was "out."

Another area in which we find the same data perceived in different ways is politics, both national politics and the internal politics of a company. For example, when we see an argument between a trade union and a management team, we judge which side looks and sounds "right" to us depending on which side we are on already. Or consider the newspapers we choose to read. We like to think that we read unbiased news, but we usually read those newspapers whose interpretations support our own bias.

We notice these different ways of viewing the world at work, too. For example, we might have disagreements with our customers over the interpretations of shipping arrangements simply because they focus on delivery dates and we look at the cost of transportation. Or, in a planning meeting, the sales director may be working with the short-term mindset of the next six months, while the marketing director is working with the long-term mindset of the three-year strategy.

Excited Mindsets

Some of our mindsets are so strong that they distort our perception of reality. For example, we may have had the experience of buying a car that we thought was special and unusual. The next day, we may have noticed this particular car almost everywhere we looked. It is as though the manufacturer had instigated a high-profile marketing campaign and tripled the sales overnight. When women become pregnant, they suddenly see pregnant women everywhere. Or if we come across a new word and look it up in the dictionary, we notice it being used everywhere, as if it is the latest fashion. The number of cars, pregnant women, or uses of a particular word has not actually increased,

Figure 4.4. A Brainteaser.

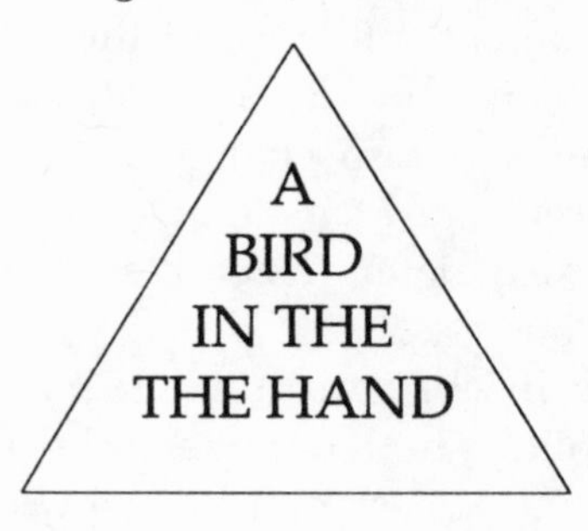

but our mind is now set to see these things, and we register incidents that before would have passed unnoticed.

Sometimes, however, a mindset can be so "excited" that in our effort to match this mindset with incoming data, we actually "see" things that are not there. Consider this brainteaser, loved by children because it plays on this tendency of the mind to jump to false conclusions. Read the saying shown in Figure 4.4.

What did it say? A bird in the hand? Not quite – look again.

The mind, which is anticipating a familiar phrase, sees what it expects to see. Because young children read more slowly than most adults and have less strong mindsets about such phrases, they are more likely to read the phrase correctly than an adult.

You may well be familiar with the following example of an excited mindset. Driving anxiously down a badly lit road at night, you may suddenly see a child about to step into your path. You brake and swerve a little, but then as you reach the "child" you see that it is only a branch of a tree, with an old rag hanging on it. Nevertheless, for a second or two the child was absolutely real for you. In times of anxiety or stress, our minds are strongly set to notice those things that we most fear, and thus we unconsciously force and twist the data until it matches our excited mindset.

Advertisers deliberately play on the phenomenon of excited mindsets. By repeatedly placing an image of a specific brand before our eyes, they condition our perception so that when we go to the supermarket, our excited mindset for that product causes that particular brand to jump out from the others. Once again, much of this process remains unconscious, and the processes by which we make our choices remain largely hidden from us.

Getting Stuck with Mindsets

Our past perception can create an excited mindset for seeing a situation in a certain way. Often, however, the facts may change over time, but we fail to see what is new because we are seeing through an old mindset.

Consider, for example, the series of eight pictures that starts with the face below and continues over the next three pages (Figure 4.5). What happens to your perception as you follow the sequence of images? Look through them now.

By the time you reached the last picture, you almost certainly had seen the image of the man's face change into the figure of a woman. But when did you notice that the image was no longer that of a man's face? Most people spot the change around the sixth or seventh picture. If we were truly seeing each picture afresh, however, we should see the change at the fifth picture. We hold on to our interpretation of the images as being of a man's face and force the new facts into this mold even though the data now better fit the image of a woman's figure.

Interestingly, when people have seen this sequence of

Figure 4.5. A Series of Pictures.

images and are then shown the images one by one in reverse, they hold on to the mindset of the figure and do not revert back to seeing the face until the third or second image from the start of the sequence, even though they know that the images will become the face of a man.

Our fixed mindsets can cause us trouble in our everyday lives. Parents easily get caught in old mindsets about their growing children, often seeing the adolescent through the mindset that they held when the child was ten years old. We may also see our partners through old mindsets. Like most people, husbands and wives change with time, but how often do we hold on to our old views and not notice the changes our spouse has made?

This propensity to hold on to a particular viewpoint occurs even at our first meeting with a person and can be preset by the smallest amount of information. For example, a class of students at the Massachusetts Institute of Technology (MIT) was about to be taught by a new lecturer. As an experiment, half the group was told that the new lecturer was "a graduate student in the Department of Economics and Social Science here at MIT. He has had three semesters of teaching experience in psychology at another college. This is his first semester teaching economics. He is 26 years old and married. People who know him would consider him to be a rather warm person, industrious,

Figure 4.5 (continued).

critical, practical, and determined." The other half of the group was given exactly the same information except for just one word. They were told that he was "a rather cool person, industrious, critical, practical, and determined."

Both groups of students then came together and sat through two sessions with the new lecturer. Afterwards, they were asked to assess his performance. Surprisingly, those who had been expecting a warm person rated the lecturer as substantially more considerate, informative, sociable, popular, good natured, humorous, and humane than those who had been led to expect a cool person, even though both groups had seen exactly the same presentations. Evidently, what the students considered to be their own individual judgments had in fact been governed by the mindset suggested to them. They had made the lecturer fit their model.

This experiment clearly shows four main principles of mindsets in operation.

1. *We create what we see.* The subjective perception of the lecturer as being considerate or inconsiderate, sociable or unsociable, humorous or nonhumorous, and so on, was something created within the mind of the student rather than existing incontrovertibly "out there."
2. *The same data can give us more than one reality.* All the students

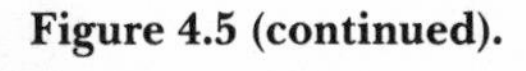

Figure 4.5 (continued).

sat through exactly the same lectures, but they saw two different lecturers.

3. *We see what we expect to see.* The information the students received had given them excited mindsets, and the lecturer they saw matched their expectations.
4. *Mindsets are self-reinforcing.* Together, the three principles above produce a self-reinforcing system. The students who "knew" the lecturer was a warm person tended to see a warm person, thus reinforcing their original mindset and keeping them stuck.

Managing Our Mindsets

We have seen how mindsets affect our perception of the world, but their influence does not end there. They have an impact on our thinking and most of our behavior.

Willis Harman, president of the Institute of Noetic Sciences in California, is very concerned with the relevance of our growing understanding of the mind to the problems and decisions facing humanity today. He writes:

> Probably the single finding with the most consequences is the discovery of the startling extent to which our perceptions, motivations, values, and behaviors are shaped by our

Figure 4.5 (continued).

> unconscious beliefs that we acquire from our early experiences and our cultural environment. . . . Once we have settled on one perception of "reality" all evidence to the contrary tends to become invisible. As they control us, they limit our creative powers and block us from fuller use of resources potentially available to us.

If our mindsets have such a powerful effect on our perception and thinking, we might well ask, Would it not be better to get rid of them? The answer, once again, is no. Without mindsets we would have no way to structure our perceptions of the world, create a coherent reality, discriminate right from wrong, bring order to our lives, and decide what to do. Mindsets are, in effect, the windows through which we see the world—and without a window we would see nothing. They are absolutely essential to human consciousness.

When people first become aware of mindsets and their influence, they often mistakenly assume that mindsets are bad. Mindsets in themselves are neither good nor bad. The real issue is whether we are in control of them or they are in control of us. We do not need to get rid of our mindsets but rather to become aware of them and take them into account, to recognize which window we are looking through.

Our minds are set from early childhood by our parents, our school, the media, our friends, and the culture in which we live. Because each of us has had different experiences, we are set in different ways; we each look at the world through slightly different windows. When we meet someone whose mindset on a certain issue is different from our own, we all too easily think that his or her mindset is wrong and ours is right. Thus, capital punishment is wrong, Communists are wrong, paternal management is wrong, or whatever else disagrees with our own cherished views "is wrong"! Of course, not all views of the world are correct, but we unconsciously assume our view of reality is the only view and are not open to what value there may (or may not) be in another's mindsets.

Mindsets give our perception a frame of reference, but they limit us insofar as that frame of reference has boundaries and what we see through it reveals only part of the picture. Thus, in managing our mindsets, we first need to become aware of which mindsets are operating in a particular situation. Then we have to ask ourselves, How does this mindset serve me, and how does it limit me?

We may, for example, hold the mindset that our children should have the best possible education. This belief serves us in that we send our children to the best school we can, support and encourage them in their learning, and make personal sacrifices on their behalf. This mindset, however, may limit us in that it prevents us from seeing that our particular view of how our children should best be educated may not necessarily work for them.

Or we may have a belief that all managers in an organization should participate in a certain amount of in-company training every year. This may serve the organization and most individuals well by ensuring that a basic level of development is sustained. However, it may stop us from appreciating that for some managers this training may not be a valuable use of time, either because their own commitment to development surpasses that which the organization offers and they would be better supported by being given time to further their development in their own way or because they are no longer open to learning and do not want to be trained.

After we explore how a mindset both helps and hinders us, we can consider the question, To what extent am I the master of this mindset, and to what extent am I its victim? When we are the victim of a mindset, it controls our seeing, our thinking, and our behavior without our even realizing it. To be the master of a mindset does not mean that we eliminate it or that we control it, but rather that we see it for what it is, a window on the world. We acknowledge how it both serves and limits us. And we take responsibility for the effects it has on us. To be the master of a mindset is to be able to choose how it influences our seeing, our thinking, and our behavior.

Figure 4.6. What Do You See Now?

5

Freeing Our Minds to Create

> To raise new questions, new possibilities, to regard old problems from a new angle, requires creative imagination and marks real advance in science.
>
> —*Albert Einstein (1938)*

Often, we do not realize the strength of some of our mindsets. Think for a moment of something about which you hold strong beliefs; for instance, abortion, nuclear defense, AIDS, drugs, religion, capitalism. How strongly are you attached to that particular belief? What would it take for you to change your mind and hold the opposite belief? Indeed, could it ever be possible for you to change? As you think about this, you may get a feel for the power and the hold that our mindsets have over us. It is this block in our thinking that holds back our open-mindedness and flexibility and kills our creativity.

We often attach so much importance to our strong mindsets that we cling to them tightly, as if our life depended on them. Some people may believe so strongly that they have to keep moving up the promotional ladder to be happy that they become neurotic workaholics and never attain the happiness they seek. Others may hold on to the mindset that personal independence is of fundamental importance and that their world would fall apart without it.

To have mindsets and to get stuck in them is the most human of traits. Most of us probably have had the experience of discovering that we have trapped ourselves with the expectation that others should do something in the same way that we do. On recognizing how ridiculous this idea is, our natural reaction is to feel bad and criticize ourselves. But this reaction does not get us anywhere; it just makes us more a victim of our mindset. On the other hand, we can, if we choose, master the situation by stepping back, smiling at how easily we trap ourselves, and beginning to practice flexibility.

We are going to get caught in our mindsets again and again and again. The sooner we learn to accept this fact and to take our mindsets more lightly, the freer we will be to look at problems with fresh eyes.

Uncovering Hidden Assumptions

So often, we approach a problem predominantly through the blinkered eyes of the past and miss possible new dimensions or other ways of solving it. We automatically bring various mindsets to our thinking, including assumptions as to what the problem is about, how we should try to solve it, the nature of the solution, or what the solution is. Most of these mindsets are unconscious, and it is often very hard for us even to see that we are making assumptions, let alone to stand back far enough to ask whether or not they are valid. These unconscious mindsets are the Achilles' heel of the manager facing the need to perform creatively.

Ralph Kilmann, in *Beyond the Quick Fix*, emphasizes the critical role that hidden assumptions play in corporate culture and decision making.

> Assumptions are all the beliefs that have been taken for granted to be true but that may turn out to be false under closer analysis. Underlying any decision or action is a large set of generally unstated and untested assumptions. If some of these assumptions turn out to be false, then the decisions and actions taken are likely to be wrong as well. Assumptions drive the validity of whatever conclusions are reached. We should not let our important decisions be driven by things that have not been discussed or considered. Assumptions need to be surfaced, monitored, and updated regularly [1984, p. 50].

Mark Brown discusses the limiting effects of mindsets and assumptions on our creativity in his book *The Dinosaur Strain.*

> So many companies are stuck with yesterday's patterns of thought. They see the world, their market, and their customers through a grid that worked some ten years earlier. Today's unprecedented rate of change calls for minds that never become set. The intelligent unset mind is what business must have and yet rigid mind-sets are more often the norm in many organizations [1988, p. 15].

A good example of how rigid mindsets can cause us to prejudge the type of solution that we look for and to miss hidden dimensions of an issue occurred in a Third-World agricultural enterprise that we were working with. As the leading tomato paste producer in its country, the company was very concerned about maintaining its market share in the face of strong competition. The senior management team assumed that poor marketing was the essence of the problem. Consequently, they analyzed their current marketing strategy in depth, looked for areas of weakness, explored how to improve the strategy, and brainstormed new ideas. After this work, the team was well on its way to implementing a new marketing strategy.

But the managing director felt hesitant. Something was not quite right. At first, he could not identify his unease. Then suddenly out it came—an almost heretical statement: "Our product is simply not of as good a quality as our leading competitor's, and people know it."

Everyone present realized that he had put his finger on the real problem. They were then able to see their hidden assumption about marketing. They had been correct in judging that their product was losing its image, but the root cause was product quality, not marketing. They all realized that in the back of their mind they had known about the quality issue, but since the whole discussion had focused on marketing, the issue simply had not surfaced. As soon as it was on the table, the team set about dealing with the real problem.

Sometimes the assumptions we hold may be valid in themselves, yet still may prevent us from seeing important dimensions of the issue. Thus, becoming aware of our correct assumptions is as important as becoming aware of those that are false.

When working with management teams on projects, we encourage them as part of the preparation phase to map out all the elements of the task, including everything that needs to be considered. Having done this, they then look at how the data are connected and explore some of the underlying patterns and implications. At this point, people are usually so caught up with the task that they do not see some of the basic assumptions on which the project is founded.

The director of an international shipping corporation wished to expand his business by establishing an emergency air ambulance service. He wanted to start this business partly to serve the large number of the company's own employees stationed abroad and partly to diversify the company by providing a service to other international groups operating in the same countries. He commissioned a research study on the project, which confirmed that this was a financially viable business opportunity. Having made the decision to go ahead with the business, he and his colleagues began to plan the implementation of the service and looked at aircraft needed, technical support and personnel required, marketing strategy to other companies, and capital investment plans.

Working with him, we began to look for some of the implicit assumptions behind this project. To tease them out we asked a series of "why" questions around each of the main areas of the project, and in particular around the central theme. We asked him, "Why is it important to have landing rights in central Brazil?" He answered, "Because one of our main potential customers has its biggest mine there." "Why is it important to service this customer?" "Because this customer will open the door to business throughout the world." "Why do you want to do this business in areas of high instability?" "Because that's where employees are most vulnerable and most in need of a service such as ours. And that's where we can really maximize our return on investment." A critical assumption around which the whole project had developed was this assumption that an air ambulance service would be profitable in these areas.

The assumption was not necessarily incorrect. However, holding this assumption as an unquestioned fact prevented the director from seeing other dimensions to the project that needed to be considered. Once he had recognized that financial viability in these countries was an unquestioned assumption, some of the dangers associated with the venture became apparent. He saw the high risk of flying in these countries, the difficulty in getting charges repaid from some of the countries, some unexpected costs of running a mini-airline, possible maintenance problems, and possible competition from unexpected sources.

Interestingly, none of these issues had been taken into account in the research study, which had only considered the market opportunity. The assumption that the business could be viable had hidden these other considerations and, paradoxically, posed a threat to the profitability of the project. By considering these other perspectives, the director was able to create a much more balanced and feasible venture.

This process of repeatedly asking why is a key to teasing out hidden assumptions. It encourages us to look more fully into an issue and discover our deeper beliefs. As in the previous example, these assumptions may be too narrow, shrinking the area in which we search for a solution.

Brainstorming

Another approach to stepping beyond the assumptions we may bring to a problem is the use of what is commonly known as *brainstorming*. In brainstorming, people spark each other's imaginations with large numbers of spontaneous and wild ideas and often think of novel solutions that none of them would have thought of individually. A fundamental principle of brainstorming is that the participants must be nonjudgmental, particularly of ideas that the rational mind says cannot work. It is these crazy ideas that can often trigger less crazy ideas, and these in turn may trigger workable solutions that would never have been suggested had the group only stuck to sensible ideas.

To loosen up the group's thinking, it is often useful to include people in the group who do not know very much about the problem and who are not therefore so "set" on the type of solutions that will or will not work. Participants are encouraged not to be serious and not to judge whether or not an idea has any value. All ideas are written down, and people are encouraged to build upon each other's ideas.

Basic brainstorming has many variations, and each can be useful in helping a group come up with new solutions to a problem. Most variations of brainstorming, however, have an inherent limitation in that they do not get people to step out of all their mindsets about the problem they are working on or the sort of solutions they are working toward. As a result, the group may miss many new ideas. Also, some people find it hard to suspend judgment on the crazy solutions. The "serious" problem-oriented part of the mind often says, Yes, but this is just a crazy solution, and it won't lead anywhere. Thus, some people hold themselves back from gaining the fullest value from the brainstorming session.

A New Technique for Problem Solving

In our own work with management teams, we have gone a stage further than traditional brainstorming techniques by adapting processes developed by Mark Brown and others. In our process, participants do not even try to solve the problem facing them. Instead, they work on a completely fictitious and crazy problem, but one that does bear similarities to the issue at hand.

Defining the Essence of the Problem

We first have people formulate the problem clearly and in an open-ended manner that does not preclude a particular type of solution. One manager had initially thought the problem facing him was that of creating new management positions for some of his bright young engineers. But when asked why, he replied, "So that I can coordinate the activities of a multidisciplined design team." How to achieve such coordination is clearly a much more open-ended formulation and one that could lead to a broader spectrum of new ideas than the problem of creating new management positions. Another person, trying to solve the problem of "poor communication," redefined the problem and made it more specific by reformulating the problem as the question, How can I facilitate greater communication and feedback through a large hierarchical corporate structure?

Defining the Zany Problem

After the group formulates a succinct and open-ended problem, they think up a new fictitious problem that has no direct bearing on the problem at hand but that does have a similar underlying nature. Thus, the problem of how to coordinate the activities of the multidisciplined design team might be "translated" as, How does one get a pile of rocks to sing in tune? And the problem of how to facilitate greater communication and feedback through a large hierarchical corporate structure might be turned into the question, How does an octopus gather in grains of gold dust? These may seem to be ridiculous and unreal questions, zany and far removed from the real problems, but that is their value. Because the problems are so far removed from the real problem, the group members are less likely to be judging (either consciously or unconsciously) whether or not a particular idea is really workable. However, the fictitious problem must bear some general parallels to the real problem.

Analyzing the Zany Problem

The group begins to solve the fictitious problem by listing all the possible causes for this problem—all the reasons why a pile of stones does not sing in tune or why an octopus has difficulty gathering in gold dust. The reasons do not have to be realistic because, after all, the problem itself is no longer realistic. The more crazy the reasons are, the more free the mind will become of the shackles of the original problem. Never had singing lessons, crushed voice boxes, fear of looking foolish, and being stone deaf are all "good" reasons why a pile of rocks cannot sing in tune. A good-humored and relaxed group will usually come up with dozens of good reasons for the fictitious problem.

The more humor there is at this stage the better. It is not unusual for a group to be doubled up in laughter for an hour or more as they become progressively looser in their thinking and come up with funnier and funnier analyses of the problem. People often remark that they have never laughed so much in their lives—and they sometimes have sore stomach muscles the next day to prove it. (Other groups in the same hotel or training center wonder what can be so funny about a creative thinking seminar.)

Finding Solutions to the Zany Problem

The group then takes each reason it has listed and tries to find one or more solutions to it. For example, to help deaf rocks hear, the rocks might be fitted with high-powered hearing aids. Or to overcome their fear of looking foolish, they might first be polished. Again, humor is crucial; becoming too serious only limits the number of possible solutions the group will come up with.

By the time this phase is finished, which can often take an hour or two, participants have usually become so involved in the fictitious problem that the real problem is far from their mind. Sometimes, they need to be reminded that all this craziness and laughter have been for a purpose: to find new approaches to the original problem.

Triggering Ideas for the Real Problem

Next, the group uses its solutions of the fictitious problem to trigger ideas for the real problem. Thus, the idea of fitting the rocks with hearing aids may trigger the idea that the design team's desktop computers be linked through a communications package, or that they all use the same software, or that the director should seek clearer ways of expressing his intentions. The idea of polishing the rocks may lead to the suggestion that the team should attend training sessions in interpersonal skills, identify and smooth out conflicts between individuals, or highlight the unique qualities and talents of each member so that these attributes can be utilized for the team as a whole. What is important at this stage is not to translate the fictitious solutions directly back into possible real solutions, but to mentally savor each one and see what new insights they trigger.

Testing the New Ideas

After listing all the possible solutions to the real problem, the group moves into the working-out phase of the creative process. Now, at last, is the time to discard all those solutions that clearly have no hope of success, to keep on hold those that may be worth looking into further, and to identify those that look as if they could offer potential solutions. Five to twenty ideas may fall into this last category, and of these, three-quarters may be ideas that would have been arrived at by ordinary problem-solving approaches.

The value of this approach is in the ideas that it generates. The approach encourages us to let our unconscious minds come through and also ensures that we do not let our mindsets block our thinking. The more lightly that we take our mindsets, the less our thinking is conditioned by the past and the more we are able to appreciate the real magic of seeing through new eyes, not just in solving problems but in the creative management of the whole of our lives.

6

Creativity in Stress

My life is in the hands of any rascal who chooses to annoy or tease me.

—John Hunter (about 1790)

People are disturbed, not by things, but by the view they take of them.

—Epictetus (first century A.D.)

Our creativity is clearly related to our mental state. A mind that is rested, alive, alert, questioning, and receptive is usually more creative than a mind that is tired, tense, depressed, anxious, and resigned. Therefore, we must take care of our own state of mind and inner well-being to facilitate our creativity.

The most common and probably the most serious impediment to a creative state of mind is too much pressure and the stress that results from it. Pressure and stimulus may often be helpful in the preparation phase of the creative process and sometimes in implementation, but during the more intangible processes of incubation and insight, we need to take the pressure off to allow our inner knowing to come through.

Unfortunately, the very situations in which we most need to draw upon our creative resources are frequently those in which we experience pressure. These pressures may be the pressures of deadlines, responsibilities, other people's expectations, financial worries, domestic problems, or the difficulties of coping with a young family. Whatever their source, these pressures usually make us feel fatigued and dull rather than relaxed and open. As a result, our creativity suffers just when we need it most.

On a wider scale, the constant acceleration in the pace of societal change puts us under ever greater pressure to make quick decisions, often leading us to react from old mindsets. We seem to have no time for creativity—particularly in the very moments when we should be stepping back to draw as fully as possible upon our creative potential.

If we are to meet the challenges facing us as individuals, as organizations, and as a species, it is imperative that we not only learn how to manage our own creative processes but also learn how to cope with increasing pressure and the stress it creates. To put it bluntly, the art of stress management is going to become essential to our survival.

Stress—Danger and Opportunity

Already, the cost and consequences of stress are enormous. As well as hindering our creativity, stress has a profound impact on our health. Doctors have estimated that between 50 and 75 percent of health problems are either caused by stress or significantly exacerbated by it. Many doctors would put the figure even higher. A simple viral infection like a common cold may not at first sight seem to be related to stress. But it is now known that stress can damage the immune system. Thus, whether or not a virus can establish itself may be directly related to a person's stress level.

Stress also affects our vitality, our life expectancy, our relationships, our ability to listen and empathize, our openness to others, our physical stamina, our perception, our emotional stability, our tendency to error, and our proneness to accidents. Hardly any area of life or any person is unaffected by stress in some way or another. Stress is very much the epidemic of our times.

Although stress is a grave threat, it also contains a hidden opportunity. As we come to understand the inner mechanisms of our reactions to pressure, we shall see that stress is another symptom of a more general underlying issue: inappropriate mindsets, expectations, and assumptions. Thus, stress also offers us a doorway into our inner worlds. Through looking at the inner roots of our stress, we can begin to see more clearly how our well-being is at the mercy of the way we think and the way we see things. As we discover more about our inner dynamics, we can learn how to exercise greater choice in our responses, thus becoming the masters of our mindsets. In addition to helping us maintain a healthier state of body and mind, managing our stress can also lead to a fuller appreciation of our inner nature and help us free our own resources and respond to change more flexibly.

Our Stress Threshold

When they talk about stress management, people frequently ask if some stress may not be useful. After all, stress can make us more dynamic; it can keep us on our toes; it can focus the mind; and it can bring mental, emotional, and physical tone to our lives.

Although the question sounds simple, people differ considerably in their answers. Some agree very much with such sentiments, but others feel that any stress is harmful. These differences are partly caused by the fact that the word *stress* is not clearly defined as far as human beings are concerned. The term has been borrowed from physics, where stress is clearly defined as "the external pressure applied to an object." The resultant change in the object is called *strain*. Thus the push you exert on a plank of wood is the stress; the amount the plank bends is the strain. When we apply the word to people, however, we mix up the two terms. We use *stress* to refer both to the pressures we are under and to the effects it has on us.

In asking whether or not some stress is valuable, we are really asking whether or not some pressure is valuable. The answer to this is yes. If we did not have the pressure of deadlines, other people's demands and expectations, change, or our own motivations and standards, we would not accomplish nearly so much. We all need stress in the sense of pressure. But we do not need to have our health, vitality, and creativity suffer as a result—that is, we do not need the strain that pressure can cause.

This approach to stress can be summarized in the simple model shown in Figure 6.1. If the demands that we are subject to are low, we may feel no noticeable strain. As they increase, we

Figure 6.1. Stress and Pressure.

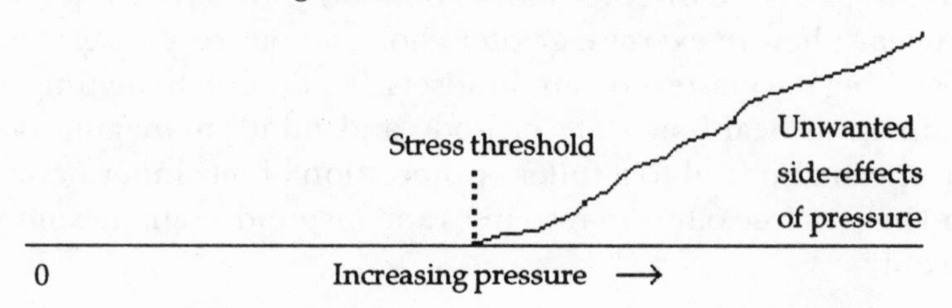

reach a critical point, beyond which we begin to experience some unwelcome side effects. It is then that we begin to feel we are suffering from stress.

This stress threshold varies from person to person. One person may easily handle a demand that for another may produce many unwanted side effects. The threshold also varies within each individual. What we at one time may experience as severe stress may at another time or in other circumstances be simply mild pressure with no side effects.

Thus, the challenge we each face is how to function under pressure without experiencing unwelcome side effects in our thinking, feelings, behavior, and bodies. How can we stay below (or not too far above) our personal stress threshold and also keep this threshold as high as possible?

The Stress Reaction

Before exploring how we might better manage ourselves, we should first look at the stress reaction itself and at the mechanisms through which pressure can lead to unwanted side effects. Of the various models that have been used to understand the stress reaction, the one that we feel is most useful and best illustrates the inner processes at work is a five-stage model. This model is summarized below and in Figure 6.2.

The demands that set off the stress reaction can come from many different situations. They include rush hour traffic, travel, noise, loss of a job, a new job, feeling criticized, government bureaucracy, time pressures, too much responsibility, too little authority, overwork, underemployment, loud music, per-

Figure 6.2. A Schematic Model of Stress Reaction.

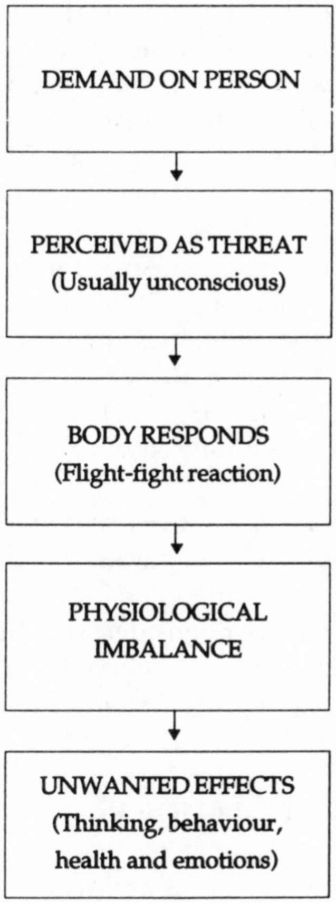

DEMAND ON PERSON

↓

PERCEIVED AS THREAT
(Usually unconscious)

↓

BODY RESPONDS
(Flight-fight reaction)

↓

PHYSIOLOGICAL
IMBALANCE

↓

UNWANTED EFFECTS
(Thinking, behaviour,
health and emotions)

sonal finances, moving, a new spouse, divorce, bringing up children, family illness or death, holidays, hunger, fatigue, insomnia, interruptions, interpersonal conflicts, thwarted expectations, being stuck on a problem, or feeling out of control. In short, almost anything can appear to cause stress.

But why are such situations stressful? You may, for example, be one of those people who find themselves becoming stressed when stuck in a traffic jam. Why is this? In some respects, you are in the type of situation you have probably been longing for all day. The phone is not ringing, there are no people bursting in with problems to be solved, and you have no papers to be processed and no meetings to sit through. You have a comfortable seat, can play music of your choice, adjust the temperature to suit you, sit back, and relax. You are warm, dry, alone at last, and with the time to think that you have been looking for all day. There is nothing about being in a traffic jam that is physically stressful (except a modest measure of air pollution).

You may find a traffic jam stressful, however, if you perceive the situation as a potential threat to your welfare, as something that may cause you difficulties and distress. You may think: What will happen if I fail to make the appointment? Will I lose face? Will I lose the contract? Will I lose my job? What will happen if I get home late for my child's birthday? What will I do if I miss the plane?

Another person, sitting in exactly the same traffic jam, may experience no threat. She may see the delay as a welcome opportunity to relax, take some time for herself, dictate a letter, think a problem through, or consider what birthday present to buy her child. She might even be relieved to have a good excuse for missing the plane. Such a person does not experience the traffic jam as stressful.

The Flight-Fight Reaction

Once we perceive a situation as a threat, our body responds automatically in the only way it knows: it goes into a *flight-fight reaction* and prepares for instant action, whether it be fleeing or fighting the threat. Adrenaline and other hormones are released into the bloodstream, the heart rate increases, blood pressure rises, breathing quickens, the muscles tense, the skin sweats, sugars are released into the blood to supply more energy, and the senses go on full alert.

Such a reaction would be very appropriate for someone who is about to be run down by a bus or attacked by a mad dog. This person would need to move instantly and speedily. However, most of the threats we experience are not physical threats requiring quick action. They are psychological threats that require little or no immediate physical action. Nevertheless, the same flight-fight response is triggered by these threats. We can find our heart thumping, our palms sweating, and our muscles tensing simply because someone has offended us, or we have to introduce a speaker at the local club, or our secretary has called in sick, or the stock market has dropped again.

The flight-fight reaction prepares us to run for our life or fight to the death. But in almost every circumstance in which the reaction is triggered, such a response is neither appropriate nor desirable. In other words, we have experienced a false alarm. So, while we get on with our day, the body has to recover and regain its normal state. This recovery may take anything from minutes to hours, depending on the intensity of our reaction.

If such unnecessary reactions occurred only occasionally, they would not present a major problem. Many of us, however, do not have time to recover from one dose of the flight-fight reaction before the next one sets in. When this pattern is repeated several times a day, the body ends up in a permanent state of emergency, although most of the time there is no emergency at all.

It is this constant reaction that makes stress such a danger to health. Virtually every organ in the body is influenced by this response. When the response continues month after month, our physical systems naturally become strained and eventually malfunction.

Moreover, there is an unfortunate vicious circle at work. The more stressed we become, the more vulnerable we become to stress. The weaker our system, the lower our stress threshold becomes. What previously would have been tolerable pressure becomes an intolerable burden and, in the extreme, can lead to breakdown. It is this vicious circle that leads the sane and rational manager to fire her secretary because the coffee is cold!

Early Warning Signs of Passing the Threshold

Clearly, if we are to successfully manage our reactions to increasing pressure, we cannot afford to wait for such serious signs of stress to appear. We need to recognize the indications of not being able to cope with pressure as soon as possible. The various symptoms of strain are many and diverse, but if we spot them early, they can be valuable signals that we have passed our personal stress threshold.

- *Physical symptoms.* We may experience physical symptoms such as headaches, indigestion, a throbbing heart, breathlessness, frequent colds or the recurrence of previous infections, susceptibility to allergies, excessive sweating, clenched fists, tight jaw, fainting, twitching muscles, nausea, tiredness, constipation or diarrhea, vague aches and pains, rapid gain or loss in weight, or rashes and skin irritations.
- *Mental symptoms.* We may find ourselves thinking less clearly, becoming indecisive, making mistakes, being forgetful, being less intuitive, losing concentration, becoming easily distracted, being less sensitive, having persistent negative thoughts and bad dreams or nightmares, focusing on short-term thinking, worrying more, or making hasty decisions.
- *Emotional symptoms.* We may experience irritability, anger, alienation, mild paranoias, nervousness, apprehensiveness, gloom, depression, anxiety, fussiness, pointlessness, loss of confidence, tension, decreasing satisfaction, meaninglessness, a "drained" feeling, lack of enthusiasm, lack of motivation, a feeling of being attacked, low self-esteem, cynicism, inappropriate humor, or job dissatisfaction.
- *Behavioral symptoms.* We may notice ourselves feeling unsociable, feeling restless, being unable to unwind, losing our appetite or overeating, achieving less, losing interest in sex (or overindulging), becoming accident prone, sleeping badly or being unable to sleep, sleeping too much, driving poorly, lying, drinking more alcohol, smoking more, muddling our words, taking more work home, being too busy to relax, being unable to manage time well, not looking after ourselves, withdrawing from supportive relationships, or experiencing increased problems at home.

Individually, any of these symptoms would not merit much attention, and we might easily dismiss it. Together, they can present us with a good picture of our overall well-being. A fairly healthy person, coping adequately with the pressures of life, may experience between five and ten of these signs at one time. A person who is experiencing between ten and twenty of these signs is obviously beginning to feel more than a healthy number of side effects from pressure. Someone who scores even higher probably needs to take his or her body's gentle warnings very seriously.

For example, one young and ambitious manager in a research department totaled over forty on the above list. As with most people who score high, he knew what was causing him so much stress. In his case, it was the uncomfortable relationship that had developed with his boss, particularly the fact that neither of them had brought the issue out into the open. He felt trapped and unable to resolve the situation, and he was resigned to a difficult work environment.

Three months later, on counting up the number of early warning signs again, he found his score had increased another five points. As one might imagine, this frightened him. It also shocked him into taking responsibility for changing the situation. After facing the issue with his boss, he managed to arrange a transfer to another division where he knew he would be supported. Six months later, his score had come down to below thirty—still high, but improving.

These signals had not only helped him tackle this particular conflict at work, they had also made him realize that he needed to deal with some deep personal issues—his own attitude to authority and relationships, his feeling of self-worth, and his sense of purpose. Using this opportunity he spent time working with himself and over the next two years came to terms with these issues.

Keeping a regular eye on these early warning signs is a useful way of monitoring your own reactions to the pressures you are under, especially as the pressures increase. The previous list can be used to take your "stress temperature" every month or so. Notice what your normal score appears to be and pay particular attention when it begins to increase. You might also note in which category you experience the most symptoms. This will vary from person to person and shows in which area of your life you are most likely to see the impact of stress.

Stress and Our Attitude Toward Life

Although we know a lot about the physiology of stress and the effects it has upon our lives, we are only just beginning to become aware of the role that our thoughts and feelings play in the creation of stress. One area in which this relationship is becoming very apparent is in our health, particularly in the health of our hearts. James Lynch, author of *The Broken Heart*, writes in his more recent book, *The Language of the Heart*:

> Medical statistics on the loss of human companionship, the lack of love, and human loneliness quickly revealed that the expression *broken heart* is not just a poetic image for loneliness and despair but is an overwhelming medical reality. All the available data pointed to the lack of human companionship, chronic loneliness, social isolation, and the sudden loss of a loved one as being among the leading causes of premature death in the United States. And while we found that the effects of human loneliness were related to virtually every major disease—whether cancer, pneumonia, or mental disease—they were particularly apparent in heart disease [1985, p. 69].

Another factor that appears to affect heart disease is our general approach to life. Nearly thirty years ago, two cardiologists, Meyer Friedman and Ray Rosenman, coined the term *Type A personality* to describe the sort of person who was always trying to do more, faster. Type As are concerned with speed, performance, and productivity. They tend to be aggressive, impatient, intolerant, hard driving, and always hurried. They are also, it was discovered, much more likely to have heart attacks.

Underlying Type A behavior is a pattern of attitudes. Type A people tend to be preoccupied with time. They are eager to get started, eager to finish, never willing to waste time, and have an aversion to waiting in lines. They also show a strong competitive tendency, set high standards for themselves, and always want to succeed and be seen as doing well. In short, they are preoccupied with efficiency and involved in a chronic struggle to achieve more and more in less and less time.

Such attitudes are not all bad. The world today needs people who are efficient, strive for excellence, thrive on competition, and make sure that things get done on time. However, these attitudes can get out of balance if the Type A person becomes a victim of these traits and lets them rule inappropriate areas of his or her life. For example, Type A people will easily become competitive when playing with their children. On vacation, they will try to pack as much into each day as possible, having forgotten how to take it easy. They have become addicted to efficiency and achievement.

Looked at from a broad perspective, the Type A pattern reflects some of the more extreme attitudes and values underlying the crisis in which humanity as a whole finds itself today. This crisis, we have seen, is fueled by an attachment to growth, a preoccupation with efficiency, a desire to be in control of the world, the deification of logic and rationality, an imbalance toward masculine values, and a reluctance to deal with emotions and the hidden dimensions of life. We could say that Western society has become a Type A society. And although we may not all be strong A-types, we probably all have areas in our life in which this pattern appears.

As the pace of change continues to accelerate, we are going to face increasing pressures to respond faster and perform more effectively. Managing our Type A attitudes and not allowing them to take control of our life is therefore going to become more and more of a necessity.

Reducing these tendencies is not, however, simply a matter of modifying behavior. People quickly find that these modifications do not last. If we are to avoid the trap of Type A behavior, we must explore and modify the attitudes and inner values that underlie this behavior pattern. A good way of doing this is to ask ourselves some simple but often quite penetrating questions that can help us step back from the mindsets that perpetuate the Type A attitude and take a fresh look at life.

What do I really want?
Why am I doing this?
What is the most important thing to me?
What is my dream for life?
What is time for?
Is this really so urgent?
What's the worst that could happen?
Will any of this matter in ten years' time?
How would I look at this if I had only six months to live?

Avoiding Breakdowns from Stress

Some people are fortunate in that they can choose to step back before the effects of stress take hold and the vicious circle winds up. Others are not so lucky. They have become so firmly caught in the grasp of stress that they are unable to help themselves.

In England, a senior civil servant working in the National Health Service had been struggling for ten years to provide a high level of patient care with a decreasing work force, reduced budgets, and an increasingly demotivated staff. At the same time, he had to battle with senior managers who did not share the same values as he had. Other people might have given up and taken a senior position in the private sector, but this choice was not on his list of options. He was very committed to his staff and to doing a thorough, professional job and was devoted to helping other people. To compound his difficulties, he was faced with personal problems. He was feeling increasingly lonely yet was so drained that he had no time for social activities. He developed workaholic tendencies and became more and more isolated.

About five years ago, he realized that he had to do something about his situation. He tried taking long holidays to relieve the pressure, only to find himself returning to an increasing work load. He restructured the responsibilities throughout his division, but that only resulted in more interpersonal problems. He attended a number of senior management courses in an attempt to learn new skills to deal with the crisis. But still his problems continued.

Throughout this period, he was perceived to be managing well and was even offered a number of promotions with additional responsibilities. Outwardly, everything seemed fine; but inwardly he felt increasing turmoil and panic. Nothing he did seemed to relieve the pressure.

After two more years, he broke down. He had a minor heart attack and was finally forced to admit that he could no longer cope. Over the next few months, as he began to step back and look at what he had been doing, he slowly began to realize that the real changes he needed to make were inner changes rather than outer changes—changes in his attitudes and his approach to life as a whole.

Peter Nixon, a London cardiologist who has spent many years studying the effect of increasing pressure on human performance, has developed a picture of the route people take through fatigue and exhaustion to the edge of breakdown (Nixon, 1982). In healthy fatigue, people recognize that they are tired as a result of working hard or lack of sleep and can redress the balance with one or two good nights' sleep. However, when people who are already fatigued face additional demands, they often assume that they can accommodate these extra pressures by pushing themselves a little bit harder. If they are not yet at the top of their curve, then their performance may well increase. But if their performance is already at its maximum, they find that rather than continuing as expected in the direction of the dotted line in Figure 6.3, their performance now goes down.

Such people enter the vicious circle of exhaustion. They become increasingly tired, their performance decreases further, they push themselves even harder, and they become even more exhausted. They become angry and despairing as they find themselves caught in a trap from which they can see no way out. They know all is not well, but they see the cause of their suffering in the world around them and other people. Victims to their condition, they find it almost impossible to take any steps to help themselves. If the additional demands are short lived, these people may return to healthy fatigue, but if the demands are maintained, their well-being steadily deteriorates, leading over the years to ill health and eventual breakdown.

Figure 6.3. Peter Nixon's Human Function Curve.

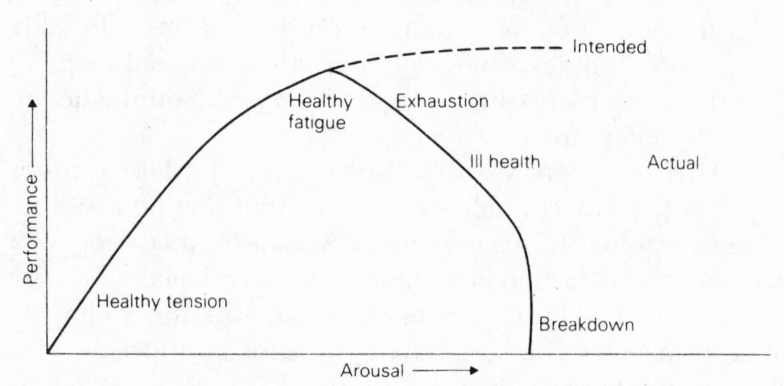

Source: Nixon, P.G.F. (1989). "Human Functions and the Heart," in *Changing Ideas in Health Care,* eds. D. Seedhouse and A. Cribb. London: John Wiley & Sons, Ltd. Reprinted with permission of the publisher.

Nixon has found that the first and crucial step before any treatment can begin is a period of prolonged sleep, often fifteen hours a day for several days. Only after this period of sleep are these people ready to step back and recognize the underlying attitudes and beliefs that have brought about this extreme condition and begin the slow process of taking a fresh look at themselves and their lives.

Although you almost certainly are not in this state – if you were, you would not have the time to be reading this – we can all learn things from this pattern. It is important to recognize our own levels of fatigue and take time to rest, rather than be in bed for weeks when exhaustion does set in. The more rushed our lives become, the more important rest will be. If we allow ourselves to be ruled by the increasing speed around us, we will become more and more fatigued. If we are to preserve an inner alertness and stability, we must balance our activity with rest. Yet the very times we need rest are often the times when it seems that we can least afford to take it. But if we do not keep this inner balance and freshness, we have little hope of becoming more creative. We will be more likely to drown in change.

Is Stress All in the Mind?

Maintaining inner stability is also a question of how we choose to see things. As was illustrated by the example of the traffic jam, the same situation can cause a marked stress reaction in one person and very little reaction in another. If we see what is happening as a potential threat to our well-being, we trigger a stress reaction. Yet, because this aspect of the process is largely unconscious, we often overlook it and think it is the external demand alone that is the cause of our suffering. Therefore, the second step in the model in Figure 6.2 is very important. It sheds light on the inner mechanisms that lie behind much of our apparent stress.

The "cause" of many of our stressful reactions is a combination of the situation we are in and the way we perceive it. When we perceive a conflict between the way things are and how we believe they should be, we may, if too attached to our belief, begin to feel threatened. It is our inability to handle this inner conflict that lies at the heart of so much of our stress.

Imagine, for example, that you are in a meeting and are interrupted by a phone call from your husband or wife, who is calling with good news: your daughter has passed her exams. If you believe this is something worth being interrupted for, you will be both pleased that your spouse called and pleased with the news. If, on the other hand, you believe that you should not be phoned during work hours except in dire emergencies, you may feel irritated and not even be able to hear the good news. There is a conflict between what is (your spouse's calling) and what you think should be (his or her not calling).

Or imagine that you are trying to catch an international flight and arrive twenty-five minutes before takeoff, only to be told that the latest check-in time was thirty minutes before departure. You can see in the lounge in front of you that boarding has not yet begun, but you are told that the desk is closed and "rules are rules." In such circumstances, most of us would feel upset, to say the least. Our mindset is that we should be allowed

Figure 6.4. How We Create Stress.

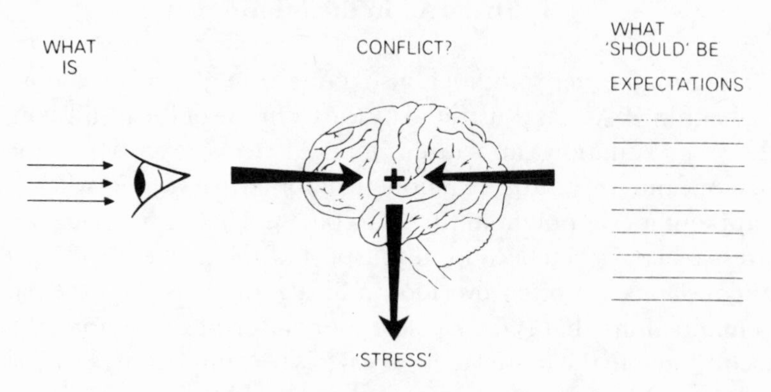

on, but the reality is different. What is and what should be are again in conflict, and we become distressed.

Or, suppose you are finding it difficult to go to sleep. You are in a warm bed, well fed, and ready for eight hours of sleep, but sleep is not forthcoming. The voice in your head tells you that you should be able to sleep, but you cannot. The more this situation continues, the more tension you create and the less likely you are to be able to sleep. Again, our perception of the situation determines our reaction.

As can be seen in Figure 6.4, the underlying mechanism of such conflicts closely parallels the fundamental mechanism of mindsets that we explored in Chapter Four. The incoming sensory data are in themselves neutral and without meaning. It is only in matching the data with past experience that we create a particular perception and meaning. Many of the situations we find ourselves in are, in themselves, neutral, but they take on significance when we try to match them with our expectations and mindsets as to how things should be. If this matching results in conflict, we create stress for ourselves.

Stress is also created when the situations we are in conflict with our deep needs and values. If, for example, when your spouse phones during a meeting, you imagine that the other people you are with will disapprove of your spouse's calling you, then the threat is exacerbated. You now feel an additional conflict between what is and your need for approval.

If the mortgage rate goes up, or even if we fear it will, our need for security may be threatened. The possibility of losing our job is almost certain to trigger stress; not only security is at stake here but very likely self-esteem as well. Flying is stressful for some people because their sense of being in control is seriously threatened. Driving a car is statistically far less safe than flying, but at least we feel more in control. We may be employed in an undemanding job and yet experience considerable stress because our need for creative expression is continually thwarted. Many of us may find ourselves stressed by the horrors of child abuse. Neither we nor our children may be directly threatened, but some of our deepest values are.

Again, it is not just the external situation that is causing the stress (although it often seems that way); it is the conflict between the situation and our judgment of it. This process and its consequences can be summarized in the following four points:

- A stressful reaction is something we create in ourselves.
- It is our perception of events, rather than the events themselves, that is the problem.
- Believing that it is the events that are responsible for the stress keeps us a victim.
- You, and no one else, are responsible for your reactions, emotional, mental, and physical.

For many people, this hidden side of our creative ability can come as a surprise. But it can also be a revelation and a release. As we become more conscious of these inner dynamics, we can take greater responsibility for them and in doing so open ourselves to a new way of managing stress.

Managing Our Reactions

Most approaches to stress management focus on managing the external causes of stress and on managing the effects stress has on us. If our production assistant is always late, resulting in considerable inconvenience and stress, we can remove the "cause" by firing the assistant who is to blame. If time pressures are a problem, we can ease the load by practicing better time management. Or if greasy food makes us ill, we may remedy this by changing our diet.

If the effect of stress is to make us exhausted, we can sleep more or practice some relaxation or meditation technique. If we are continually wound up, we may find that exercise such as jogging, swimming, squash, or even walking helps us unwind. If we bottle up emotions, finding someone who is willing to listen to us without judgment can help get these feelings off our chest.

While such approaches certainly help, they do not get to the root of the problem. As we have seen, stress is more than a simple cause-effect reaction. The inner dimension of this process, our perceptions, expectations, beliefs, and needs, are also a central element in the equation. This opens up to us another way of handling stress.

When caught in a traffic jam, for example, rather than seeing it as a threat and wishing it would go away, you could ask yourself: What is the opportunity here? What is the best use I can make of this time? By doing so you would probably experience a very different set of reactions. Maybe you would still be late, but you would be considerably less stressed. (And you might also come up with a new creative idea on the way!)

Simple questions can be useful in discovering what is really going on inside. The next time you feel upset by someone or something, you might stop for a moment and ask yourself:

- What am I telling myself that is making me feel this way?
- What is the expectation I have that is being challenged in this situation?
- Am I demanding that I should be treated in a special way?
- What am I assuming about what I need to be happy?
- Am I blaming someone or something for disturbing my peace of mind when really it is only my judgments that are disturbing me?
- What is really being threatened?

When we are under a lot of pressure we often find it very difficult to handle our emotions. When we are angry at someone for not behaving as we would like, it is very easy to place all the blame for our distress on the other person. After all, we say to ourselves, if that person had not behaved in that way, I would not be so upset. But if we had not been so attached to our expectations and projected them onto the other person, we would not have felt so threatened by his or her behavior, and the conflict inside us would not have escalated.

If we find ourselves angry at someone else we can defuse our reaction by stopping for a moment and asking ourselves: What might he or she have been thinking? How might he or she have been feeling in this situation? What past experiences could have led this person to behave in this way? What might he or she have been hoping to achieve? Asking such questions does not make the other person's behavior right or deny our own values. But if we can step back in this way, we may see the other person's behavior from another perspective, and we may find ourselves feeling compassion along with our anger.

The Creative Manager and Stress

As said earlier, the way of the creative manager is an inner way. Creative managers recognize that as well as taking care of the outer aspects of change, we also have to handle its inner dimensions—the attitudes, perceptions, and values that lead us to respond in the ways we do. Looking at the inner dimensions is also the way that creative managers cope with increasing pressures in life. As well as tending to the more tangible sides of stress, they also tend to the inner processes behind their reactions.

In a way, stress resembles the frustration phase of the creative process. If we only see frustration as a barrier to be pushed past, we may prevent ourselves from hearing what it is trying to tell us, and the frustration will in all likelihood continue. If, on the other hand, we see frustration as an opportunity—a call to step back and listen to our own inner voice—we can move beyond it and draw more deeply upon our creativity.

Similarly, if we see stress only as a barrier to our functioning, we will tend to manage only its outer forms, its causes and effects. If we see it as an opportunity to learn more about our own selves and what is really important to us, it can become another window into ourselves. Stress is a signal that we have more to learn about our inner worlds.

In seeking to manage the beliefs and expectations that lie behind stress, we are taking another step in freeing ourselves from our inner limitations. We are creating the opportunity to be more at peace with ourselves. Rather than being tossed around by the seas of change, we can learn to ride them with inner calm. As we have seen, such stability is going to become critical to our ability to handle accelerating change. If we can remain calm within and more open to ourselves, we will be able to think and act with greater clarity, creativity, and humanity.

Learning to manage our reactions to pressure is part of our daily practice as creative managers, for, in learning to handle these hidden processes, we are also learning to bridge our inner and outer worlds. Learning to manage our reactions is learning to think about life in a new way. And this is the essence of humanity's task today.

7
Social Re-Creation

There is no need to run outside
For better seeing,
Nor to peer from a window. Rather abide
At the center of your being;
For the moment you leave it, the less you learn.
Search your heart and see
If he is wise who takes each turn:
The way to do is to be.

—Lao-tze (sixth century B.C.)

Clearly, the twenty-first century will place radically different and unprecedented demands on us all. While many of the creators and managers of organizations—whether they be large or small, governmental or commercial, profit or nonprofit organizations—will bear a particular responsibility for navigating humanity through these turbulent times, the challenge will be one we will all have to confront.

Where will we go for help? Will we, like our parents, believe that by turning to experts such as scientists, engineers, politicians, and corporate leaders, we will be able to control and cope with change? Many of us know in our heart that this strategy no longer works. We are going to need help of a different order.

As we have begun to see in previous chapters, the blocks to change are on the inside rather than the outside. The more we understand ourselves, the more we can see what lies behind our fears, both conscious and unconscious. As we come to see our fears in a different light, we become more free and willing to change. Learning about ourselves thus becomes a central focus in the life of creative managers.

A New Attitude Toward Learning

For most people, learning is synonymous with education. We spend anything from twelve to twenty years of our life in schools and colleges, learning for the life ahead. We may then assume that our formal education is finished. But we also recognize that this education only partially equips us for life today.

Many of our current educational systems are based on the need to train people for a society rooted in the Industrial Revolution. In earlier times, it was important to give large numbers of people the skills and techniques appropriate to the tasks of an industrial society. Lifelong skills were required for lifelong tasks.

Today and in the years to come, we need learning that is relevant to the challenges of the information age. First, the speed of change demands that learning should be continuous and lifelong. And second, we need to learn new inner skills.

Many of the exciting new developments in learning are taking place within organizations. Faced with the pressing need to develop employees' personal skills such as thinking and planning, leadership, communication, working in groups, and creativity, in addition to the many new information-technology skills, organizations have taken over much of the task of continuing education. Some have established their own educational centers and colleges. Many support their employees in ongoing educational programs outside the company. Traditional training departments are rapidly changing their focus from specific job skills to a more general education of the person as a whole. The more progressive the company, the greater its emphasis on continuous learning. Some companies even require their managers to attend at least two weeks of educational programs every year.

This new attitude to learning is reflected in a comment from one of the captains of industry interviewed by Francis Kinsman. Speaking of the changes that will come in the 1990s, he emphasized:

> The most serious impact will fall on people who have given up the idea of learning, and for them the adoption of quite different attitudes will be a difficult and painful process. So once again, the middle-aged manager is going to feel the pinch [1983, p. 79].

This statement does not imply that all managers have given up. Many are indeed taking a fresh look at their own learning. As the managing director of a large construction corporation said, "I have realized that even though I am forty-eight years old I can actually open myself to learn. I thought I had stopped when I finished school, but now I can begin again."

In the future, we will need radically different personal skills and attitudes. In the past, we tended to assume that to change the world it was sufficient to change our behavior and to learn new and better techniques of control. Consequently, we have learned to organize and manage the outer forms of our personal and professional lives. We have learned how to read balance sheets, set up new companies, produce and market new products, coordinate international operations, use and implement new technology, and design and stage elaborate events. Yet, although we may know much concerning the world around us and how to control it, we are also recognizing that focusing on the outer world alone does not necessarily help us cope better with the more personal aspects of change. On the contrary, if we continue to react only to the external aspects of change, we run the risk of breakdown, both individually and as a society.

Historically, education and teaching have largely depended on external experts. Today, however, we increasingly recognize that learning is a process that takes place from within the person and that we need to invest the same energy and commitment we already make to outer development into exploring our inner worlds.

The Impact of Self-Exploration

Most people only consider the idea of self-exploration and inner discovery when they have a problem. Until recently, inner guidance has been regarded as the province of the therapist, the psychiatrist, and the priest. Over the last two decades, however, interest in self-development has increased rapidly, almost as rapidly as the explosion of information technology. But, being a far less tangible phenomenon than technology, our interest in self-development does not, at first, have as visible an impact.

Willis Harman regards this "human potential movement" as a new science of subjective experience with profound implications for our future. He summarizes the basic tenets of this changing image of the person in three propositions:

1. The potential of the individual human being is far greater than the models of humanity currently in vogue would lead us to think possible.
2. A far greater proportion of significant human experience than we ordinarily assume is composed of unconscious processes, including those mysterious realms of experience we call intuition and creativity.
3. Included in these partly or largely unconscious processes are images of the self and limitations of the self and images of the future that play a predominant role in enhancing or limiting our actualization of our capacities.

Harman goes on to comment that

> we have undersold man, underestimated his possibilities, and misunderstood what is needed for what Boulding terms "the great Transition." [These tenets] imply that the most profound revolution of the educational system would not be the cybernation of knowledge transmission, but the infusion of an exalted image of what man can be and the cultivation of an enhanced self image in each individual child.

It is this other dimension of learning that is so crucial to the present time, and the various paths of the human potential movement can be seen as pioneering ventures into this largely uncharted territory. Activities such as meditation, yoga, relaxation, biofeedback, counseling, psychotherapy, martial arts, and body work are sometimes regarded as symptoms of the "me" era—a narcissistic indulgence and a flight from the "real world." While there may be an element of truth in this view, it would be a mistake to believe that this is all that these activities are. They can also be seen as the responses of people from all walks of life to an inner call to understand themselves and life more fully. They are symptoms of a growing search for meaning.

Inner-Directed Values

The human potential movement is but one face of a much larger social phenomenon. Since the early 1970s, it has become apparent that, throughout the more industrialized countries, individual values and motivations are steadily changing. These changes have been the subject of a number of long-term studies, including the Stanford Research Institute's Values and Lifestyles Program (VALS), the Monitor Programme in the United Kingdom, the European International Research Institute into Social Change study, the Naisbitt Group's *Trend Report*, and Daniel Yankelovich's research. These studies have revealed that while the majority of people may still be focused on their outer, material well-being, the concern with inner values and self-direction is steadily growing and is now a significant factor in social development. Christine and W. Kirk MacNulty from the VALS and Monitor programs call this emerging set of values "inner directed":

> Inner-directed people are motivated by self-actualisation. They are largely unconcerned about the opinion of them held by the world at large; their criteria for success and the standards of their behavior are within themselves. This does not imply withdrawn or reclusive behavior. Indeed the inner-directed individual usually has a broad horizon, a good understanding of world events, and a high tolerance for other people's behavior [1985, p. 334].

In his book *New Rules: Searching for Self-Fulfillment in a World Turned Upside Down*, Daniel Yankelovich talks about the same trend, although he puts it slightly differently:

> Americans are weighing the rewards of conventional success against less lucrative but more satisfying personal achievements and are seriously considering the latter.

Kirk MacNulty describes the emergence of an "inner-directed" population over the past thirty years as

> . . . a natural phenomenon, the result of an evolutionary process, if you like. Like the enquiring, intellectual experimental researchers (nascent physical scientists) who emerged from the religiously orientated society of mediaeval Europe, the Inner Directed population does not appear to be the product of any of our social institutions. . . . Like his scientific predecessor, the Inner Directed [person] fits as uncomfortably into the materialism of the Industrial paradigm as Galileo fitted into the dogma of the church [1985, p. 363].

The emergence of these new values can be seen as part of a much older historical trend. For centuries, the dominant need was for sustenance and survival, and the majority of people spent their waking hours working the land. The new technology and economics of the Industrial Revolution provided the opportunity for greater material well-being and release from the drudgery of a survival-driven existence.

Over the next two centuries, great numbers of people became concerned with creating a more comfortable physical environment. Increasingly, they had the means to improve sanitation, housing, clothing, food, transportation, communication, medical care, and schooling and the means of producing more and more goods to facilitate these changes. These changes provided the platform for the emergence of a consumer-driven society.

People's dominating motivations shifted away from sustenance and survival toward personal security and material well-being. People became, in the language of the VALS and Monitor programs, more "outer directed" in the sense that their motivations were increasingly dominated by a need to improve their social position. This motivation has led to a society in which many people are driven by the need to be seen and recognized by others, a need that often gives birth to the belief that financial and material well-being are all-important.

Freedom to Explore Our Inner World

Today, however, new opportunities are opening up to us, and another shift in personal values is becoming apparent. It is now rapidly becoming obvious that the values of the industrial era—work, physical security, material development, and economic growth—are no longer appropriate. Important as they have been for raising the quality of life and personal welfare, these very values now threaten our continued collective well-being and survival. In addition, work as we have known it is becoming redundant.

Information technology is freeing many of us from the drudgery of work. Robots are taking over factory production lines, computers have replaced rooms full of account clerks, and word processing has transformed the publishing industry. Soon, voice recognition and high-level software will put traditional secretaries out of work; expert systems will take over much of the routine in medicine, education, and scientific research; computer-generated film will put Hollywood in a briefcase; sales-driven data banks will replace marketing departments; and artificial intelligence will reduce the need for lawyers, accountants, civil servants, and many of the other workers intrinsic to the industrial society. Hardly any professions will not be dramatically affected, if not eliminated, by the Information Revolution. Perhaps as much as 75 percent of work as we know it today may well be eliminated or transformed by the turn of the century.

To some people, these changes may seem most undesirable. In the short term, the changes will clearly bring a painful disruption to many people's lives, and much will need to be done to help people through these difficult personal transitions. Society as a whole will face a challenge far greater than the one that was posed by the Industrial Revolution, for these changes will shake the very foundation of our economic system.

One natural response is to try to hold back the tide of change and seek ways to return to full employment. We should not forget, however, that the reduction of work has been our goal for centuries. The history of the industrial age is the history of labor-saving devices. From the early days of steam engines, water pumps, and cotton looms, we have progressed to the production of washing machines, dishwashers, vacuum cleaners, food processors, electric can openers, toasters, power drills, car washers, automated gas pumps, take-out and convenience foods, electronic bank tellers, self-driven lawn mowers, electric golf carts, and a wealth of other inventions designed to minimize unnecessary work and give us more free time. Now, with the extraordinary and unprecedented freedoms that information technology is bringing to us, we may be approaching the point where many of us do not have to work at all.

But what is all of this growing freedom for?

Faced with a rapidly changing world in which so much of what we have held to be important is falling away, we find our old values beginning to wane. People are asking themselves: What is deeply important to me? What is it I truly care about? What do I really want to do with my life? These questions are not just another manifestation of the selfishness that so dogs our current society; they are a fundamental reevaluation of the values by which we live. We are asking ourselves how we want to be rather than what we want to have. We are trying to set our own standards rather than deriving them from what others tell us or from how others behave. We are trying to be true to ourselves rather than being overconcerned with appearances and status. This is the essence of the shift toward inner-directed values.

What is more, this is the first time in our history that it has been possible for large numbers of people to follow these inclinations. Previously, it was only possible for a privileged elite to do so. Now, having created more time for ourselves, we have the freedom to ask these fundamental questions. Furthermore, our high quality of life and material well-being today give us greater opportunities to follow these inner promptings and make them a part of our daily living.

In short, we are being freed to explore our inner worlds, to develop our thinking, and use our mind in a different way. Perhaps this is the real revolution and the hidden opportunity behind the information age.

8

The Inner World of the Creative Manager

"Trust thyself." Every heart vibrates to that iron string. The great have always done so. We now must accept the same transcendent destiny.

—Ralph Waldo Emerson (1841)

People today increasingly are asking themselves what it is they really want to do. For some, this questioning dawns slowly; for others it can come as a sudden shock. We may ask this question both at times of great happiness and joy and also at times of crisis and personal suffering.

We may have had the experience of our job suddenly being eliminated, for example, or we may know of a friend or relative to whom this has happened. For some people, this occurrence may bring deep despair and hopelessness, leading them to some fundamental questions about themselves and their lives. Other people may see the change as an opportunity to do what they have always wanted to do and may use their newfound freedom to give their life more meaning. Many people have chosen not to continue with a business career but to work in the helping professions, where they may find less pay but greater satisfaction. Others have decided to dedicate themselves to trying to preserve the environment.

Facing death can be another crisis that brings us up against such questions. Whether it be through having a heart attack, discovering we have cancer or another major illness, suffering a serious accident, or simply coming to terms with our own mortality, our life may be suddenly brought into sharp focus, leading us to take a fresh look at our values and priorities. We may also be moved to look at the purpose and meaning in our own life and reconsider the opportunity our life presents us with when faced with the death or deep suffering of someone close to us.

A similar personal reevaluation can sometimes happen when we seem to be doing well. After having achieved considerable material security, professional success, and personal recognition, we may for no apparent reason find ourselves feeling bored, frustrated, without purpose, and perhaps depressed. Our initial reaction may be to try to modify our external situation. We may try to exchange our "boring and unsatisfying" work environment for a "more interesting one" or even change our job. We may change our home for a "better" one. Or we may think about changing our partner and seek new relationships.

More often than not, such reactions are only ways of avoiding the more disturbing questions that face us, and very little is resolved. If we are to move beyond the crisis rather than simply patch it over, we must turn inward and face ourselves. Our frustration and discomfort should, once again, be seen as a call from within. It is the voice of our own self reminding us to listen to a deeper truth.

As we saw earlier, society as a whole is facing a very similar existential crisis. We are being forced to challenge many of our assumptions, to look at the world in new ways, and to reconsider our priorities. In this respect, we are all undergoing a crisis of values. Every one of us is being asked to listen to the voice within and to let it speak through our decisions and actions.

The Voice Within

What is the voice within? It is the part of us that feels that something is not quite right, tells us when we are pushing too hard, recognizes that we did not treat someone fairly, senses that something is going on behind another's words, and tells us that we should hold back a while rather than rushing in.

The voice within is also that part of us that tries to tell us what is best. It is the inner knowing that tries to speak to us in our dreams. It is the intuition that leads us to call a friend at the right time. It is the feeling that there is more to life. It is the urge to follow a higher purpose.

Although this voice is within us all at all times, it is not always easy to hear. The clamor of the world around us is so much louder. Moreover, our externally oriented society conditions us to believe that our inner voice is not real and not to be listened to. Its counsel often goes against all that convention would have us hear.

Nor do we have many skills or techniques with which to hear our quieter intimations. Most of the skills we have learned are skills that help us handle the world around us more than the world within. They are of little value when it comes to managing our inner processes. To cooperate with the intangible, we do not need techniques so much as self-understanding, self-trust, and a willingness to stop "doing" and just listen.

As was apparent from our exploration of the creative process, it is this willingness to listen to our own inner worlds that is the mark of the creative manager. We need to listen to ourselves to know where we are in the creative process and where we should go next. We need to listen to our frustration to hear what it is trying to tell us. Is the voice that says, "I can go no further," telling us that it is time to do something completely different and incubate for a while? Or is our feeling of not getting anywhere a sign that we have not done enough preparation? Only we know. There are no rules to follow in the creative process—except the rule of listening to and trusting our inner voice.

Of all the phases of creativity, insight most of all demands that we respect our inner truth. It is, quite literally, an "in-sight," a time when we suddenly "see" a new connection, a new way through. The whole of the creative process is centered around this moment when our deeper knowing breaks through. For example, Kekulé already knew the answer to the problem of the benzene structure, but he needed to turn off his questing mind, relax, and float in dreams before his subconscious could speak to him. Of course, the inner voice is not always right. Like any aspect of our mind, it can be fallible. This is why testing and evaluating are also crucial parts of creativity. The value of learning to listen to this inner sense is not to arrive at incontrovertible truth but to open ourselves to another aspect of ourselves beyond our normal thinking. When we are open to this voice, we often find that its deeper guidance contains a wisdom that our conscious thinking was unable to reveal.

The Language of the Mind

In order to understand our "inner tuitions," we first need to recognize the language of the mind. Seldom do the deeper levels of the mind speak to us in words. They communicate more often in images, sensations, dreams, and feelings.

Verbal language is, from an evolutionary perspective, relatively new to the human brain. Sensory imagery, on the other hand, is much older and more fundamental. As a result, most of us remember sounds, smells, and sights more easily than phrases or sentences. The smell of new-baked bread transports us to the kitchen of our childhood. We dream in pictures rather than words. When we think of tomorrow, it is usually images that come to mind. We may have warm feelings as we imagine the reception awaiting us as we return home from a long trip. We may sense our hunches in our body. Even as you read these examples, your mind was very probably turning them into images of one form or another.

Such imagery may not always be vivid or photographic. Nor need it be only visual; the other senses can speak to us just as clearly. Yet, in one form or another, imagery is nearly always in our mind. (If you believe you are a person who does not easily create images, then, whatever happens, do not now imagine a green door—anything else but a green door! Or the sound of someone knocking on it!)

To hear our inner voice, we should therefore listen for the language that the mind uses to speak to itself rather than the language that we use to communicate with other people. One helpful way of doing this is to symbolize our inner knowing as a wise person.

Sometime when you have half an hour to yourself, find a quiet place where you will not be disturbed, settle down, close your eyes, and take some minutes to relax. Then imagine yourself in a garden and allow images to float into your mind, however they may come. Listen to sounds, imagine textures, and watch any visual images. After a few more minutes, imagine that you see a wise person coming toward you. Again, allow the images of this person to come freely; do not try to force the person to look or be any particular way.

After you become acquainted with this wise person, you might try asking questions on subjects about which you would like some guidance. Listen to what he or she has to tell you. Maybe the person has something to show you; again, words are not always the most appropriate form of communication. You may want to ask this person if there is anything else that he or she would like to bring to your attention. The answers may be surprising, but often they are just what we need to hear but could not hear until we gave our inner voice a symbolic form.

Another important value of imagery is its ability to take us beyond our crystallized mindsets. Many organizations are beginning to use images as a way of seeing past the outdated, mechanistic, and one-dimensional view that has shaped their corporate cultures. In his ground-breaking book *Images of Organization*, Gareth Morgan (1986) shows how organizations of the past are often described with images of machines, although images of brains and brain processes or trees with their branch-and-root systems can be used as metaphors that evoke a more alive and creative view of the organization and the complex issues it faces.

Mindsets and Inner Needs

Our mindsets about what should or should not be, or about how we should or should not behave, can often stand in the way of our hearing our deeper knowing. Earlier, we saw how our mindsets can restrict our thinking and creativity by leading us to make false assumptions and how, by holding on to these assumptions, we may see threats that do not really exist and so limit our creative response to pressure. We have also seen the influence that mindsets exert on the value systems that characterize an age.

Our approach so far has been one of accepting our mindsets. Accepting them does not make them right or wrong, but by acknowledging them and the role they play in our thinking and perception, we can take greater responsibility for the effects they have on our decisions and behavior. Sometimes, however, we may become aware of mindsets that are inappropriate and that we would like to change or be without. What do we do then? We cannot simply wish these mindsets away; we formed these mindsets for good reasons.

Recall the image of mindsets as windows through which we view the world outside. Like any window, they can be looked through the other way, from the outside in. This is what we must do if we wish to change our mental habitual patterns: we must look back through the window into our inner worlds and explore the beliefs and attitudes that lie therein.

Behind most of our mindsets is an inner need or motivation. We may believe that money is important because it helps satisfy our need for security. We may assume that by telling others how to behave we will be able to exercise more control over them. Or we may have a prejudice against another person because he or she threatens our desire for recognition and approval. In these examples, the need that the mindset fulfills is fairly apparent, but this is not always so. Often, the need is much more difficult to see. In most cases, we are not even aware of our underlying needs, let alone know how they influence our mindsets.

The relationship between needs, mindsets, and the behavior they generate is well illustrated by a situation that occurred during a creative management program we were running for one of our U.S. clients. We came down to breakfast early to prepare for the day ahead. The vice president of one of the divisions was already sitting at a table on his own. Out of courtesy, we explained that we needed to talk together and excused ourselves from joining him. "That's okay," he replied. But as we were walking away, he added, half-jokingly, "But don't expect me to buy you a drink tonight!" We both felt this was a rather odd and unnecessary remark but said nothing.

Later that day, as part of the program, we were looking at the needs and values behind mindsets and how they affect our behavior. During this session, the same vice president, somewhat embarrassed, asked how our model would explain what he had said at breakfast. He had also felt that his reaction had been rather immature. Moreover, he recognized that this behavior was a common pattern for him, and one he did not like.

As we explored the mindset that lay behind this particular behavior, it became clear that he did not fully believe that our reason for wanting to sit elsewhere was so that we could plan our day. He was telling himself that we wanted to avoid sitting with him and were rejecting him.

What was behind this assumption? He began to realize that he wanted to be recognized and approved of by others and to feel that he belonged to the group. Beneath these needs was an even stronger need to be loved, not in the romantic sense, but to be accepted and appreciated as a human being. In excusing ourselves from sitting with him, we had unknowingly (to him as well as ourselves) posed a threat to these needs, leading him to feel rejected.

He then saw that these needs lay behind not just this particular incident but also many other similar responses. They made him vulnerable, especially in situations that could be interpreted as rejection. His habitual behavior in response to this mindset had been to attack and reject others. And he used humor to hide it.

As he began to understand this mechanism, he saw that both the mindset and his reactions were totally inappropriate for an adult, even though when he was a young adolescent they had served to protect him. What is more, these mindsets seldom brought him the love and recognition he desired. More often he created a self-fulfilling prophecy and was indeed rejected.

What was missing was the ability to acknowledge his needs to be recognized, to belong, to be loved and to take responsibility for his emotional life. Once he began to look back through the mindset to discover what was behind it, he could relate to these needs more directly and take steps to modify his behavior.

Our behavior, mindsets, and needs constantly interact and influence one another. We tend to believe that the outer environment determines our behavior. Although this may be partly true, our behavior is also determined by our inner environment, our own personal needs. Our needs might include the need for security, control, approval, nourishment, love, recognition, belonging, self-actualization, stimulus, creative expression, and so on. There is nothing whatsoever wrong with these inner needs. They are always there, and we are always trying to satisfy them. They are fundamental to our life as human beings and part of our inner reality.

Changing Our Mindsets

The person in the previous example found it relatively easy to uncover the need that lay behind a particular mindset. But for many of us, uncovering these needs can, at first, seem to be a perplexing task. We do not know quite what we are looking for, and, in addition, we have to look for it in the dark. The situation is rather like the first time we used a computer. We knew very little about how to work with it, yet, just as handling the computer became easier with time, so too can we become more familiar with our personal needs and how they operate in our lives.

We can often help ourselves uncover the needs behind our mindsets by asking ourselves questions such as the following:

- What am I afraid would happen if this mindset were not there?
- What do I fear I might lose if I let go of this belief?
- When and why did I create this mindset?
- What does this mindset help me get?

You personally may find some of these questions more useful than others and some easier to answer than others. You may also find that other questions are more helpful to you. The purpose behind all the questions is to get at what is anchoring a particular mindset in place. By looking at the answers that come up, you can probably begin to get a feel for the need that is operating. It may help you to look back at some of the needs listed earlier. Do not be surprised if you find that more than one need is at work.

Simple questions such as these helped a factory supervisor understand and change a disagreeable behavior in his domestic life. Occasionally, his fourteen-year-old daughter would stay out late drinking with friends. Although he did not object to alcohol in itself, his initial response was to get furious, lose his temper, and confiscate her clothes and makeup. After a few days, he would become contrite and apologize for what then seemed extreme and unjustified behavior. But try as he would, he had been unable to respond differently when the situation recurred.

By exploring the thinking that lay behind his behavior, he fairly easily uncovered the mindset. He believed that by taking away his daughter's clothes and makeup he would keep her at home and so prevent her from staying out late drinking. To discover what needs this mindset was serving, he tried answering questions similar to those listed earlier: What did he fear he would lose if he let go of this belief? The feeling of being in control of his daughter. How did this belief help him? Because of his love for his daughter and his sense of responsibility, he did not want her drinking at this early age. He wanted to have some influence over her behavior.

Once he saw what was motivating his irrational reactions, he realized that he could satisfy his need to influence his daughter in other ways. He sat down with her, treated her more like an adult, talked about his own concerns, and worked out a better solution with her about appropriate boundaries for her at this stage in her life.

In short, it is not our needs themselves that cause us problems but rather the mindsets we hold concerning the best way to satisfy them. Ways of meeting a need that may have served us earlier in life can, over time, become ossified mindsets. Rather then helping us meet our needs, such attitudes often stand in our way. If we can recognize our deep needs and listen to what they are telling us about ourselves, we can often find better, more appropriate ways to address the needs. In effect, we release the anchor holding the mindset in place and give ourselves a much greater choice in how we think and act.

Other People's Needs

After we discover the needs behind some of our own behaviors, we tend to assume that other people follow the same pattern. But this may not be the case. Compare the needs of the person who drives fast because of a need for excitement and stimulation with those of a person who drives fast because driving wastes time. The behavior is the same; the needs are very different.

The difficulty in knowing which particular need underlies a behavior is a problem faced by any organization trying to motivate its staff. For example, a large software house was having difficulty retaining some of its brightest young programmers. It was spending a great deal of time and money training them, only to have them leave after a year or two. The company was paying these people top salaries, providing excellent work environments, and offering fringe benefits beyond the industry norm. But still, people kept leaving.

The mistake that the senior managers had made was to assume that these people were motivated primarily by material needs. When they took time to investigate what their people really wanted, they found a strong need for personal autonomy, creativity, and self-expression. But the size and complexity of the projects the programmers were working on required teams of ten or more people and provided little opportunity to satisfy these more personal needs. In most of the companies that the young staff members were moving to, the projects were small and the teams more intimate, which allowed a greater expression of individual creativity.

Another example of misunderstood motivations occurred some time ago on a tea plantation in India. The owner decided to increase his workers' motivation by doubling their wages. The result was that the workers turned up half as often.

Our Common Search

Beneath all these various motivating forces is one motivation that we all share. Whatever we do, we do because we hope that in one way or another it will either reduce internal discomfort or make us feel better. Put very simply, our underlying goal is a happier state of mind. This is our most fundamental motivation.

We eat because we know we do not like feeling hungry. We may seek promotion because we believe it will make us happier. We may try to do a job well for the satisfaction it brings us. Some of us listen to music in order to feel at ease. Others seek solitude because they think it will give them peace of mind. We may help others because it gives us a sense of fulfillment. A few even commit suicide because that seems better than continuing to live with the burden of oppressive emotions. Whatever we do, we are seeking to increase our inner well-being.

The basic needs mentioned earlier are also fueled by this search. We may believe that having security will give us peace of mind, that receiving recognition will bring us happiness, that being in control will give us a sense of freedom, that a sense of belonging will make us feel better, or that self-actualization will bring fulfillment.

Yet we also know in our heart that these beliefs are not necessarily true. We know of people who have all the security they could dream of and still are not at peace; people who have achieved considerable recognition, but who have not found inner fulfillment; and people who have control, influence, and power beyond measure, yet still are not happy. What we so easily forget is that it is not security, recognition, or control we really want, but peace of mind.

Recognizing this fact in our daily life is crucial to achieving the happiness we seek. Here again, some simple questions can be of help. Whenever you find yourself attached to the idea that something or other is necessary for your inner well-being and happiness, you can try asking yourself,

- If I do not get what I want, can I still have peace of mind?
- Even if I do get what I want, will it really bring me peace of mind?

You may believe that only by reaching your sales target will you be able to feel happy at the year's end. But is that really true? You may tell yourself that if you do not receive the promotion you have sought you cannot be content. Or you may think that your partner has to behave in a certain way for you to be happy. But is any of this really true? Even if all of it were true, would fulfillment then be yours?

It is important to recognize that we always have a choice. We can choose how we perceive and judge a given situation and hence choose how we respond to it. If we see things as a threat—a threat to a mindset of what we must have in order to be at peace—then we will not be at peace. On the other hand, while it may not be easy, we can always see things in other ways, as opportunities rather than threats.

We have the choice to see things in different ways at every moment of the day. The more we learn how to exercise this choice, the more we can become the master of our thoughts, feelings, and behavior, which will leave us more free to respond creatively to the situations in which we find ourselves.

9

The Creative Manager with Others

No one is wise enough by himself.

—*Titus Maccius Plautus (about 200 B.C.)*

Creative managers are not just concerned with their inner realities: they are men and women of action. As such, they inevitably interact with others, and through this interaction, the power and influence of their creative impulses are magnified.

Working with others enables us to go beyond our personal weaknesses and limitations. It allows us to draw upon resources that are beyond the means of any individual and to move from personal endeavors to large-scale operations. This group effort is the foundation stone of any organization. Thus, important as it may be for us to develop our own inner resources, it is equally important for us to pay attention to our relationships and to support others in their creative process.

Creative Relationships

Although we are each individuals, we are not creatures of isolation. We are always relating to other people, whether at work, at home, or in our social community. These relationships may range from intimate personal relations to more formal business relations and from contacts we make every day to those that we make only very occasionally. Yet, important and ubiquitous as our relationships may be, most of us find them one of the most difficult areas of our life. Few people would say they have no room for improvement in this arena.

Many of us treat our relationships as something "out there" that we have little influence over. They are good, bad, or indifferent, and that is that. Often, people blame the state of the relationship on the other person. They fail to see that the quality of our interaction is our mutual responsibility. In this respect, a relationship is something we create; it is something in which the creative process is always present.

Our relationships may at times be frustrating. One of our colleagues may not behave as we would like, we may not understand a customer, or we may feel that we are not heard. Relationships go through many periods of incubation when we are apart from our colleagues and the acquaintance is no longer in our thoughts. We have moments of insight when we understand more clearly another's reality, see why the person is as he or she is, and experience a closer connection. We continually "work out" our relationships by resolving misunderstandings, integrating differing needs, and exchanging new ideas. In addition, everything that happens between two people can be seen as part of a continuing preparation for future interaction.

When we do pay attention to the quality of our relationships, it is more often than not our more intimate personal connections that we focus on. Yet it is equally important to nurture and care for our professional relationships, for they directly influence the quality of our work. One of the captains of industry interviewed about the future of business in Francis Kinsman's *The New Agenda* put it this way:

> The importance of interpersonal relationships is a peak thing and good managers of people—*people people*—will be badly needed throughout business. The revolution in communication means that there will be a block between the older generation managers and a new generation with these new skills. . . . This is not only a matter of pure communication but actually something closer to consultation and togetherness—the feeling of oneness [1983, p. 59].

This view was echoed by another corporate leader, Robert Staubli, president of Swissair, at a European symposium on long-term questions of the future:

> There are sound reasons for emphasizing—some might say over-emphasizing—work on the capability of community.

> In a company, the estimated loss of potential in performance ranges from 30 to 50%, due to interhuman problems, unsettled conflicts, inhibitions, troubled relations, insufficient freedom, and a lack of opportunities for development. I think this estimate is cautious [Staubli, 1986].

Working at our relationships is not easy. Like many other of the less material and less tangible aspects of our lives, we are taught very little (if anything) at school or college about this art. Most of us grow up with little awareness of the care and attention that our relationships require. Then later, as we come to realize the importance of working on them, we probably find we do not have the necessary understanding and interpersonal skills to do so. We do not know how to take responsibility for our relationships. Sometimes we believe the other person should be more caring. At other times, we live in hope that our relationships will work out well more or less of their own accord. But this seldom happens.

Communicating

The essence of any relationship is communication. It is communication, in one form or another, that links people together. It is the fabric of human society.

The word *communication* comes from the Latin *communis*, meaning "common" or "shared." In its original sense, communication is the creation of a common understanding, a sharing of experience, between people. This sharing can take many different forms. We may share agendas, strategies, objectives, problems, wishes, news, and even idle gossip. We may share past experiences, ideas and insights, hopes and fears, and feelings and emotions. We may share in words, in body language, in the looks we give each other, in the tone of our voice, and also in what we do not say. We may share through music, art, dance, and all the other expressions of our creativity.

Yet it is surprising how careless we can be over something that is so important to our lives and work. We are usually very careful with something that is physically shared, like property, a company, or money, yet we show far less care when it comes to sharing our thoughts and emotions. Too often, a communication does not result in a shared experience. It more often can be described by a statement such as this one: "I know you believe you understand what you think I said, but I am not sure you realize that what you heard is not what I meant."

Communication, being a flow of information between people, involves us as both senders and receivers. Improving the quality of our communication, therefore, requires that we pay attention both to what we send and how we send it and to how well we receive what others send us.

Sharing Our Feelings

Much of what we share in our interactions are our ideas and experience. We tell of what has happened to us, share our learnings, explain our thinking, ask questions, give answers, show our intentions, supply information, direct others, convey our wishes, and so on. But this is not all there is to communication. Communication becomes richer and far more valuable if we can create an atmosphere of openness, trust, and mutual respect so that we can also share our more personal thoughts and intimations, feelings and emotions, hopes and fears, vulnerabilities and misgivings, deeper wishes and aspirations, feelings of anger and frustration, sensitivities and intuitions, excitements and joys, and ideals and truths. True communication involves the sharing of any and all of life's experiences, in both verbal and nonverbal ways.

Increasingly, people are appreciating the need for deeper forms of personal communication. Yet many are also discovering that this is not easy. If our interaction with another person hitherto has been largely in terms of facts and figures, goals, strategies, performance, and agreements, we may find it very hard to start talking of our feelings.

Underlying this difficulty is the fact that most of us do not even have the right vocabulary to express our feelings. It is surprising how often a manager, when asked how he or she feels about something, replies, "I think," followed by some judgment or assessment: "I think it is useful for us" or "I think it shouldn't be allowed." It can often take some time before he or she realizes that these are not feelings, but thoughts. When the person finally understands the difference between expressing thoughts and expressing feelings, it may still take some inner exploration before he or she can find the right words: "I feel frustrated that this meeting hasn't achieved what I expected," "I feel resentful that. . .," "I feel expectant," "I feel uncertain," or "I feel joyous."

Learning to express our emotions can take a lot of practice. Even when we have the vocabulary and know what it is we are feeling inside, it is not always easy to share our feelings with others. We may fear being embarrassed, looking foolish, or appearing soft, or we may be afraid of the other person's reactions. Yet sharing feelings can be a most valuable step in almost any area of business. In the case of the chemical company mentioned in Chapter Two, only after people had expressed their emotions could they resolve their conflicts. Although at the level of ideas, the people in the company were polarized, they had feelings in common. But they had to share their feelings before they could see this.

Telling the Truth

Perhaps the most important lesson in communication, and the lesson many of us have to learn over and over again, is always to tell what is true—although this does not mean having to tell everything. Not being open and honest about our feelings may seem to get us through short-term difficulties in a relationship, but it does not help in the long term. If we do not communicate what is true for us, then we can hardly expect the quality of our relationships to remain high. The vice president of personnel in an American retail company expressed this idea very clearly:

> So many of these guys hide their tensions. We haven't woken up to the fact that hiding them is more of a threat than exposing them. Getting them to talk about why they feel uptight in the same way that they talk about the budget figures, the margins, the marketing strategies, and the

> training that they just attended is the hardest thing. The problem is being prepared to take the risk and expose the soft underbelly. It all comes down to being honest with each other.

Being truthful does not mean that we always say things that we know others will find hurtful or share everything that is going on inside us. But it does mean not saying things that are untrue. If, on being asked how we are, we say okay when we know inside that we are not, we are not telling the truth. We are just taking an easy way out, and, more often than not, the other person knows it. It would be more honest to say, "I'm less than okay today, but I do not feel I can (or want to) talk about it at the moment."

Nor does telling the truth mean that we have to blurt things out directly and, often, clumsily. We should take care over the process. If, for example, we want to tell somebody an uncomfortable truth, we can often make it far easier for ourselves (and for the other person) if we first share what is true about how we are feeling. We might say, "Look, there is something I need to talk about, but I'm finding it very difficult to get started and I'm afraid of how you might react. I'm also not sure that I can express myself clearly, and I'm concerned that you may not understand me properly." This is just as honest as blurting out the uncomfortable facts. By first sharing our emotional truths, we open up the way we relate and usually find it easier to then talk about the more difficult issues.

Communicating these hidden, deep truths is essential to working effectively together in groups. Employees are increasingly demanding full and truthful communication from their boss, their colleagues, and also from themselves. Although they want a warm and friendly environment, they also want one in which honesty is valued. They want to see difficult issues on the table, not hidden and unspoken or glossed over with half-truths. Summarizing his survey of senior management, Francis Kinsman writes:

> Managers will have to be more communicative to the workers, exposing their own vulnerability and their mistakes and making themselves responsive to the employees' minds. A subsequent growth of mutual respect will mean that things are easier to do in the long run. But before they do, it will be necessary for managers to show their humanity first. Can management dare to show its personal problems and be open with the workforce? And if it does will the workforce dare to listen? The answer is yes, yes, yes [1983, p. 58].

Colin Marshall, chief executive of British Airways, speaking at the Institute of Directors in London, put it even more succinctly: "Always tell the truth—it usually is rather effective." It may not always be easy, but as the inventor/architect/philosopher Buckminster Fuller observed, "If everyone spoke the truth, and only the truth, all of the time, there would be no problems in the world."

Disclosing our unspoken thoughts can have other advantages. One of us recently got together for an afternoon with two colleagues to discuss possible ways of continuing our work together. Just as we were about to finish one person said, "This idea keeps coming into my mind. It sounds silly, and it probably won't work for you two, but what if we go away together for a few days to explore some of the things that are exciting to us and then invite some of our corporate friends to join us and run a spontaneous program that is right on our cutting edge?" The other two of us instantly approved of the idea. By honoring her inner voice and expressing her feeling, however silly it may have seemed, this person had come up with the most exciting idea of the afternoon. As our friend Ray Gottlieb has often said, "Declare your hidden agenda; it may be the best idea around."

Listening

Inept as most of us may be at expressing our feelings, we are even worse at receiving what others have to say. Sometimes we do not even hear the words another is saying, let alone understand the real intention behind them. Usually, we are more interested in the messages we are sending out than we are in receiving the messages sent to us. Yet good listening is essential to any communication and to any relationship.

As with poor expression, the costs of poor listening are high. Michael Ray and Rochelle Myers point this out in their book *Creativity in Business*:

> For the lack of listening, billions of dollars of losses accumulate: retyped letters, rescheduled appointments, rerouted shipments, breakdowns in labor management relations, misunderstood sales presentations, and job interviews that never really got off the ground [1986, p. 76].

Moreover, it is not just listening to the words that is important; we must also learn to understand what is behind the words. There was the senior manager in the National Health Service mentioned earlier who felt that his colleagues had never really understood his difficulties. Marketing managers may feel that the latest product line will not sell well but because they cannot express their hunches easily, withhold their hesitation until it is too late. Many people say that they are okay but really mean the opposite.

Take for example the managing director of a British manufacturing company who had for a long time been concerned about one of his general managers. The general manager repeatedly said that everything was fine and that he was coping well. The managing director had taken his words at face value but had failed to hear the underlying message. When he finally did hear the message, he was very troubled by what he found:

> Now, for the first time, I'm beginning to understand how he feels, and I'm realizing how stressed he is. He has always been so positive and committed to the company and would carry out all the directives he was given. But the communication has all been one-way, from us to him. There's been no listening to him. Now we've got to act fast; otherwise it is clear he could become a very sick man.

We know that communication is a two-way process, involving both sender and receiver, yet we often behave as if good communication were only a question of being an expert and polished sender. Listening skills are something that few of us are taught. It is far easier to teach the skills of clear expression, for these, being things that we can *do*, are tangible skills. But good listening is not something we do as an activity; it is more an attitude of mind and an exercise of our attention. It is an inner process and therefore much harder to handle.

In this respect, listening bears close parallels to the inner phases of the creative process. Preparation and implementation are things we can do, and our training has given us various skills and techniques to manage these phases. Managing the frustration, incubation, and insight phases is, however, much more difficult. They are more mysterious, far less tangible, and much harder to teach.

We work with these inner phases not by doing so much as by stepping back and trying to hear inwardly what it is we are trying to tell ourselves. We are listening to our own inner voice. Therefore, it is not surprising to find that the qualities of mind so important for these aspects of creativity—receptivity, relaxation, and an open mind—are also keys to listening well to others.

Listening and Self-Talk. As with creativity, our mindsets often get in the way of our listening. They appear as *self-talk* that goes on inside our heads. Self-talk is not the quiet inner voice that we discussed in the previous chapter. It is a much louder, far more conscious voice that interrupts our thinking. It is the voice that wants to add to what is being said, that says, "Yes . . . but . . ." and starts composing our own response. It is the voice that wonders, What's his hidden agenda? Did he understand what I said? Is she getting at me? Should I close the deal now? When will they finish? It is the voice that wishes we had not started this conversation, that thinks, I bet he's been talking to my boss, that suddenly remembers we must call somebody.

At times, this self-talk may be useful, but it can also interfere with our listening. We can only focus on one thing at a time. So long as our attention is taken up by the voice in our head, we are not fully listening to the voice of the other person.

We can often reduce our level of self-talk simply by becoming aware of it. Noticing that we have gone off on an inner tangent can be enough to wake us up and return our attention fully to the other person, assuming, that is, that our intention is to listen. If we are being truly honest in our listening, we might even interrupt the speaker to say, "I'm sorry. I wandered off for a moment. Could you please repeat that last bit just so I can be sure I got it?" Although most of us would find such an admission an embarrassment and prefer to be less active in our listening, few speakers find it offensive. More often, they appreciate our willingness to hear and understand.

Our self-talk can be another window on ourselves. Much of it comes from some inner fear. We may be afraid that we may not have the chance to express ourselves, that we are not in control, that the other person may not approve of us, or that we will not get what we want. Most of the time, these fears are irrational; they only arise because some mindset or need is threatened. Noticing the kind of self-talk that repeatedly comes up for us in conversation allows us to step back and become more aware of our deeper mindsets and needs and be less at their mercy. Thus, somewhat paradoxically, although our self-talk may block our listening, truly hearing what it is telling us can free us to listen more fully to others.

Giving Feedback. When listening, we should remember that we cannot know whether or not we have understood without giving feedback. A person may ask us, "Have you understood?" and we may reply yes, believing that we have, but how do we know? Have we heard what the person really meant? The only way to find out is to give feedback.

Before we respond to what the other person has said, we might say, "Let me just check that I've got it right. What I heard you saying is . . ." and then briefly summarize in our own words what he or she has said. Again, this is something that many of us find difficult, mainly because it is not something that people usually do. But giving feedback invariably leads to clearer communication and often nips misunderstandings in the bud.

Giving feedback frequently seems totally unnecessary. When asked to do so as an exercise, a manager we know was very reluctant to engage in feedback to his boss. "I know what he's saying," he said. "It's simple to understand, and he's said it to me before."

Yet when he did eventually feed back what he thought had been said, he was surprised to hear his boss reply, "No, you haven't heard the most important bit." It took several exchanges before the manager was able to summarize the message to his boss's satisfaction. Had he not done so, the hidden misunderstanding would undoubtedly have continued to interfere with their relationship for a few more years.

In addition to ensuring that a communication is clearly received, giving feedback also improves our listening skills. Our intention to summarize the other person's point of view can be a major help in focusing our attention on what the other person is saying. Our intention to hear will be much greater, and the voice in our head that much quieter.

In making this effort to listen more deeply, we are in effect saying, "I want to hear you," "I want to understand you better," "I want to appreciate what is true for you." Not only does this effort enhance communication, it can also have a dramatic effect on the quality of the way we relate. As we begin to hear other people more fully and are in turn heard better by them, we often discover not only the differences between us but also the range of common ground we share.

Building Teams

At a deep level, we are all very similar. We are each seeking to improve our feeling of inner well-being. We all have values that we want to express in one way or another, and we all have needs that we are trying to fulfill, although the nature of the needs may vary from one person to another. We all have mindsets, some that help us and some that get in our way. We each experience pressure but respond to it in different ways; some may see a demand as a welcome challenge, while others may see it as a major threat. Similarly, the process of creativity is fundamentally the same for each of us; yet we each have areas in which we are strong and confident and others in which we are less confident.

Valuing individual differences is a key to successful management, as Ralph Kilmann brings out so clearly in *Beyond the Quick Fix*:

> The most enlightened managers today are those who take pride in reaching out for help from whomever they can get it. These managers know their limitations and accept them as part of their human makeup. They are the first to recognize what they can do effectively by themselves and when they need to enlist the aid of others. It is not a matter of massaging egos – it is a matter of doing what is necessary to solve complex problems. The enlightened manager looks for diversity of inputs as a natural and recurring part of his job [1984, p. 25].

As the problems we are required to tackle continue to become more and more complex and interrelated, teamwork becomes more and more of a necessity. Letting go of our mindsets about independence can be difficult, however. For example, the new head of a growing seafood company had been struggling to find ways of bringing his organization into line with the needs of the 1990s. The old-style managing director of a small seafood company had to be "all things to all people." He was the buyer, production manager, and salesman. Today, the rapidly changing marketplace and the increasing pressures the industry is under meant that he needed to build a team with specialized skills.

> We have a much more complex set of problems than we had 15 years ago. EEC fishing regulations, Japanese fish farming, the dumping of stocks, the increasing sophistication and discrimination of the consumer, and new marketing practices mean that I can no longer plan the business on

> my own. I must now draw on the skills of our senior management team.
>
> None of us can do it alone. We can't even come near, even though we sometimes think we can. We not only have to work together, we depend on one another. Our skills are different and we each bring something different to the party and that's what makes it possible. We need the humility and courage to recognize our limitations and make it work for the company as a whole; otherwise we won't survive for long.

The recognition of the need for teamwork pervades all organizations and all levels of management, from the top to the factory floor. Team building figures high on most internal agendas, various experiments have been tried, and important insights and practice have been gained in understanding how teams work. Different theories and models have been developed for building teams; a variety of methods now exist for exploring individual roles and team profiles. Yet despite this continuing investment of time and energy, for many people, getting a team to work well together is still a mysterious process.

Although much of the work on team building has gone a long way in giving us an understanding of the complex social and interpersonal issues at play in teams, deeper personal issues still need to be addressed. These issues are seldom voiced and are difficult to observe. Even when they are voiced, they may not fit easily into the models.

We often regard these more elusive and puzzling human traits as unnecessary weaknesses and personal foibles. We expect people to act without hidden agendas or personal needs; that is, to be a perfectly rational team member. Unfortunately, such perfect team members do not exist.

The current models for building teams are not necessarily wrong, but they are incomplete. It is important to learn to manage the more unpredictable human processes that are to be found in every team.

The Human Face in a Team

Attending to these more mystifying dimensions can, as we have seen, be a much more challenging task than managing the more familiar and tangible aspects of a group. This fact was brought out very clearly during our work with a client's senior management group. Over a period of twelve years, the president of the corporation had built up a team of able and experienced people, each committed to the company. They knew each other well, recognized each other's strengths and weaknesses, and realized that working together as a strong team was important. But in recent years, something seemed to be missing.

The president's solution was to take the team to the mountains for a few days. There they could all have a good time together, away from the demands of the office, and come to know each other a little better. At the same time, they could decide on next year's corporate goals and long-term strategies and so create a renewed sense of team spirit. With us there to run an exciting program and fire the team with enthusiasm, the president believed he had a good formula for success.

Around lunchtime on the first day, however, it became clear that much more would be needed. Body language, tone of voice, odd remarks by some, and silence on the part of others, suggested that a lot was not being said. With some gentle encouragement, the hidden feelings slowly began to come out, and their appearance surprised many of the group, particularly the president.

They clearly knew each other well in terms of their experience, expertise, abilities, likes and dislikes, and how each would be likely to behave in a particular situation or respond to a specific challenge. But there their acquaintance stopped. They did not really know each other in terms of what was important to them and why they behaved in the way they did.

One of the more surprising things that emerged concerned the financial director's attitude toward the president over an issue that had happened ten years previously. The group all knew of the past disagreement, and everyone thought that since the issue itself had been resolved and never spoken of again, the rift had been healed and forgotten. On the surface it had, but not in the financial director's mind. Although the disagreement was no longer a big issue for him, he still felt that he had been misunderstood and wronged all those years ago and feared a repetition. His fear was not something that he lost any sleep over, and he saw that it was probably irrational and unjustified given the current circumstances; but still it was there in the back of his mind, preventing him from feeling completely at ease with the group.

Unexpressed fears such as these are incipient poison in any relationship. It always seems easier to keep quiet and avoid either looking foolish or upsetting someone else. Yet the very fact that these fears are withheld creates a separation between the people concerned.

Part of our role was to create a safe environment in which the financial director would not feel judged and the others would be open to hearing him. With some difficulty, he began to talk about his concern with the rest of the group. As he did, he found that it was not the fear of a similar event recurring that was standing in his way but the fear of appearing irrational to the rest of the team.

The group was somewhat surprised to hear that he still, after all those years, held a mild resentment toward the president. The president himself, who thought that all had been forgotten, was particularly surprised. However, the group did not react with criticism and rejection but rather relief. Now they could understand why the financial director sometimes behaved oddly in meetings. His behavior was not just a result of a personality quirk; there was a reason behind it.

By sharing more of his inner world, the financial director included himself more in the group. And the more that his colleagues understood him, the more they were able to open up to him. A more significant result, however, was a major transformation in his relationship with the president. The two men were able to heal the past in a way that had not been possible as long as part of the past had been kept hidden.

Once the financial director had shared his own concerns, others in the group were able to talk more freely about themselves. One was able to talk for the first time of her need for security and how that affected so much of her life, including her work in the company. Another, who had always been the quiet member of the group and whom the president had taken to be a less strong team member, began to speak of his shyness and then of his vision for the company, revealing a commitment to his work far deeper than anyone had suspected.

The group did not end up having the exciting "gung-ho" time they had expected. Instead, they began to see that what was really missing from their team was true communication. Their time together became a time of group discovery and the development of a deeper mutual understanding and personal caring. It provided the foundation for a far more solid team.

Managing the Team Process

Managing a team is not always as easy as it was in the above case. More often, it is an ongoing process with its own frustrations, learnings, and breakthroughs. Rather than taking teams away to the country to fire them with enthusiasm or for heart-to-heart meetings, team leaders often need to develop a sustained awareness of the human concerns present in any group of people and the ability to handle the team process.

Within the more subtle and personal dynamics of a team, we again find elements of the creative process at work. People do not usually work together well as a team immediately; they generally need an initial period of preparation and settling in. There are periods of frustration and discomfort as people begin to find their place together or hit unresolved issues. At times, individuals may need to work on their own; at other times, the whole team will need to take a break and "incubate." For facilitating insights and breakthroughs, a receptive environment is important. And there are times of intense activity when some, or all, of the group members are actively involved in "working out."

As with the creative process, there is much we can do to facilitate the inner aspects of the team process.

- Set aside time at the beginning of a meeting for people to talk briefly about how they are, what they are feeling, and, when appropriate, their hopes and fears and any issues they may be struggling with. Do not force this disclosure but concentrate more on creating an environment where this is possible.

- Do not rush straight into the agenda. Recognize that any group, however well acquainted they may be, always needs some time to "come together." People need time to settle and feel at ease; they need to feel heard and accepted as part of the group. The less often they meet and the less well they know each other, the longer this process will take.
- Get the hidden human agendas on the table. Although this may seem to take up valuable time, it is an investment that repeatedly pays off. You are creating a climate within which the team will work far more smoothly and tackle more effectively the official issues on the table. You may feel that talking about agendas is opening a can of worms, but if there *is* a can of worms, the sooner it is opened and the worms released the better—they can do far more harm hidden in the can.
- Remember that the best way to encourage others to talk about personal issues is to talk about any concerns and feelings you may have. Put your own hidden agenda on the table.
- Above all, handle other people's personal feelings and concerns with the sensitivity, care, and compassion with which you would like your own feelings to be handled.

Because it is unfamiliar to most of us, managing the inner process of a team is difficult and often seems like working in the dark. But if we are to find the key to getting team members to work well together, we have to look in the dark as well as where there is light. Thus, creative managers are not just charismatic leaders, although they may sometimes take on that role. More important, they also manage the people and the process of the team, thereby enabling the individuals in the team to manage their own inner worlds.

Creative Teams

Because the creative process takes place within us, we tend to think that it is something we do on our own. Yet the process requires of us a range of skills and abilities: from analytical and rational thinking to imaginative and visionary skills; from the capacity to step back and see things calmly in perspective to the dynamic, pragmatic skills of the implementer; from the ability to discover and challenge our assumptions to the willingness to listen to our inner knowing.

Few of us excel in all of these areas. Some of us are good at seeing the essence of a problem, some at stepping back and seeing where we have become stuck, some at coming up with new ideas, and others at testing or implementing proposals. Clearly, if we are to draw upon our creative potential to the maximum and express it fully in our work, we also need to draw upon the strengths of others.

The ways in which a group can pool its individual creative skills has been explored in considerable depth by K. Meredith Belbin at the Henley Management College in England. Belbin was concerned with forming teams that would be good at creative problem solving. Initially, he put together people who scored high on conventional creativity tests. Yet these teams, full as they were of "creative" people, were disastrous at solving problems.

The reasons for this failure are clear once creativity is recognized as a process involving several different phases. Most creativity tests implicitly assume that creativity is about coming up with new ideas. Thus they usually identify "original thinkers," who are good at the insight phase. Such people tend to be individualists; when several of them are put together in a team, they are all ideas but no action. No one listens; they are all too busy putting forward their own solutions. Thus there is no one to focus the group, to evaluate which ideas are worthwhile, and to put the ideas into practice.

Clearly, a truly creative team needs to be able to handle all the phases of the creative process. Besides people who generate ideas, a team needs good leaders, researchers, implementors, and team builders. Over fifteen years of research with hundreds of teams in a diversity of industries, Belbin (1981) has found eight different roles that individuals can play in teams.

1. *The plants, or the original thinkers.* These are the people who score high on most creativity tests, the "idea generators." Belbin calls them plants because in his early research such people were "planted" into teams to see if they would enhance team creativity. They often seem withdrawn and quiet, but they are usually thinking and will suddenly come out with very original ideas.
2. *The resource investigators.* These people also bring new ideas into a group, but the ideas come from their interaction with others rather than "out of the blue." Much more sociable than the plants, they tend to be out and about, talking to people, seeing what others have done, reading, and picking up new ideas from others and developing them.
3. *The chairman.* He (or she) coordinates the efforts of the team to meet external goals and targets. He sees others' strengths and weaknesses and makes sure that all voices are heard. He keeps the process of the team in balance, welcomes contributions, listens well, sums up, and, if a decision is to be made, makes it firmly on behalf of the group. But the chairman may not necessarily be the team leader.
4. *The shapers.* This is another leadership role, complementing that of the chairman. Shapers often are dominating, extroverted, "follow-me" leaders. Always keen to get into action, they want to pull others along with them. Self-confident and results oriented, they give "shape" to the way the team's effort is applied.
5. *The monitor-evaluators.* As critics rather than creators, the contribution of monitor-evaluators is the measured and dispassionate analysis of proposals. Sometimes resented by plants and shapers for their "Yes . . . but . . ." approach, they are the ones most likely to stop the team from committing itself to a misguided project.
6. *The organizers.* Also called "the company workers," the organizers are disciplined and turn concepts and plans into

practical working procedures. Give them a decision, and they will work out a schedule. Give them an objective, and they will produce an organizational chart. They work for the good of the company rather than the pursuit of self-interest.

7. *The team workers.* Sensitive to other people, the team workers are aware of individuals' needs and concerns and perceive clearly the emotional undercurrents of the group. They are good listeners and communicators and encourage others to be the same. They are the facilitators of the team process.
8. *The completer-finishers.* The completer-finishers guarantee delivery of an objective. After a decision is made, they like to be sure that all the details have been checked and that everyone knows his or her responsibilities. They are fastidious, conscientious, and thorough. They make sure that deadlines are met and preserve a sense of urgency in the group.

As you look at these descriptions, you can probably see yourself in several of them. It is not that one of us is a "chairman" and another a "team worker"; we each possess most of these characteristics to some extent. It is important to become aware that different roles exist and to see which roles tend to be strongest for us and which are weaker.

In addition, the roles we play will be different in different groups. A person may appear as a strong shaper in one team but may be much less so in another team where an even stronger shaper is present. Such an analysis is valuable in understanding the role a person takes in a particular team rather than categorizing a person in a fixed way.

Belbin makes it very clear that there is no formula for designing the perfect team. Successful teams can vary in size from two to ten or more, and many different combinations of team roles are possible. Where his work is most useful is in helping us understand why a particular team may not be performing very creatively, as in the case of a group of original thinkers, a team without any original thinkers or resource investigators, or a team with too many shapers pulling against each other. This analysis can also be very valuable when putting a team together to ensure that all aspects of the creative process are adequately covered.

This sort of evaluation was crucial to a project group in a medium-sized industrial company. On completing the self-assessments that Belbin has developed (1981), they found that the team was very strong in the roles of original thinker, resource investigator, chairman, team worker, and completer-finisher. But no one was performing the role of monitor-evaluator. Without someone in this role, the team was very likely to set off on paths that had not been properly tested and assessed, only to find out months later and at great cost that they had acted precipitously.

Seeing this lack, the project leader enlisted the help of a good monitor-evaluator from another division to sit in on the team's monthly meetings. This person's task was to listen to their suggestions, bring to their attention any factors that they might have overlooked, and point out areas in which he felt they were being unrealistic.

Attending to how people work together as a team is an important step in allowing our creative impulse to flow more effectively into the world, but our work with others does not end there. If we are to be as effective in our work as we would wish, we need not just the support of others but also their fullest creativity.

Empowerment

Every one of us is part of a larger organization, whether it be our family, project team, social community, company, or even our species. The changing times we live in and the new challenges ahead will require that these and other organizations are able to respond with as much creativity as possible. Therefore, the creativity of as many individuals within these organizations as possible must be released. If we are to see our visions and values become more manifest in the world, in our work, and in our families, it is not enough to become more creative managers ourselves; we must also seek to help others become the same.

Management can be defined as "optimizing the use of the

resources available." In terms of managing people, this translates as facilitating another person's development, seeing that individuals use their own potential to the full. In other words, an essential ingredient in any management of people, whether at work, at home, or socially, is to foster the individuals' own creative processes; that is, to help them understand their own inner worlds, trust themselves and their insights, communicate what they truly feel, see their own mindsets and step back from them, be aware of their own hidden motivations, and, perhaps most important if we are all to pull together, be in touch with their hearts and their sense of what truly matters.

Before we jump into trying to help others release their own creativity, however, we should remember just how difficult it is to do this for ourselves. We cannot tell ourselves to be more creative; it is not something we can make happen. This book has tried to show that we must learn to let creativity happen.

This does not mean that there is nothing we can do to facilitate our own creativity; there are many ways in which we can open up the flow of this innate and most human of impulses—as this book also has tried to show. Becoming more creative is something that grows upon us as we become more aware of ourselves and our inner processes, something that Abraham Maslow saw thirty years ago when he wrote that creativity and self-actualization are very closely linked and may even turn out to be the same thing.

The same is true when we turn our attention to releasing the creative potential of others. It is no good telling people to be more creative; we cannot *make* others creative nor can we make them *let it happen*. But we can do a lot of things to help them exercise this power for themselves.

Take for example the creative process itself. It is relatively easy to help others in the more outward-directed phases of preparation and implementation. We can teach skills and give feedback on performance for these phases. But when it comes to handling the more inner-directed phases, we need to take a somewhat different approach.

Another person's frustration is part of his or her own process and not something he or she should be admonished for.

Rather than advising someone to snap out of it and get on with the task, we should accept the validity of the experience for this person and remember how we have become frustrated ourselves.

However, we should also be aware of the temptation of projecting our own experience of frustration onto this person by suggesting, for example, that he or she take time off to incubate. This person may need something very different. We can give him or her the space to concentrate on how he or she is feeling at a particular time and to hear what the inner voice may be saying.

In similar ways, we can encourage others to take their own time for incubation and insight by, for example, not chastising subordinates for "wasting time" when stepping back from the problem for a while may be just what they need and not judging or rejecting another's insight because we cannot immediately see its value. Once again, it is not so much a different way of "doing" that is required of us but a different attitude, a different way of "being" with others—a way that lets others feel empowered rather than judged or threatened.

Helping Others Empower Themselves

Empowerment is one of those often-used but much misunderstood terms. We cannot empower others, much as though some of us would like to. Empowerment is something that we create for ourselves. It is a sense of freedom we feel inside, a freedom to be who we really are, to draw upon our own resources, and to express our own truths. When we feel empowered we feel alive, alert, in touch with our feelings and sense of self-worth, responsible, valued, and free to choose.

But no one empowered us. No one makes us feel that self-worth, just as no one ever *makes* us feel upset, even though we sometimes believe that these feelings come from outside. Feelings of empowerment are feelings that come from within, from our own self. Similarly, if we want those we work and live with to feel more empowered in their own lives, we cannot do it for them. What we can do is create an environment in which they can empower themselves.

The following are some things we have found helpful in facilitating this environment. You may well have other things you would like to add to this list.

- Honor the dignity and integrity of every person. Beware of judging others just because they think, perceive, or behave in ways that are different from your own. Allow them the freedom to be their own unique self. This does not mean that you have to accept their views or actions as correct; exercise discrimination fully. But do not judge their worth as a human being. No one has that right.
- Encourage others to express their feelings and communicate their own truths. And listen to what they have to express. Remember, we all need to be heard.
- Take time to talk to people. Do so in your own way and a way that they will understand. Trust your own inner voice about how to be with people rather than your mindsets or how convention dictates.
- Recognize that others have their needs, too. Appreciate that their resistance to change may be as deeply personal as yours. Put yourself in their shoes. Try to experience how they might be seeing things, what their beliefs and assumptions might be.
- Trust yourself and be yourself. Your own self-honesty can liberate the same in another. If you do not know the answer, do not pretend you do. Ask colleagues, subordinates, and bosses for their input. Value their views and contributions, and so will they.
- Do not lead others to believe they "should" do something. Self-talk such as "I should," "I ought to," and "I have to" can inhibit our inner freedom.
- Do not think of the old way as bad. What you or others did before is not wrong, just not appropriate now.
- Remember that deep inside our wants are much the same.

Working on empowerment is not always easy, especially when people expect that a good manager should tell them what to do. An example of this attitude was brought out in a meeting we had with a senior manager and members of his team. When questioned on how he saw his role, he replied:

> I am the lubricant. That's my role as general manager. My priority is the effective development of human communication, the proper understanding of our objectives, and how we can develop people to achieve their potential within the division. In doing this, we'll realize our business goals and have fun together doing it.

Some of the people in his team did not think this was a sufficient answer and kept pushing him to be more specific. Interestingly, he remained unmoved. He kept referring them to this notion that he was the "lubricant" of the group. These were not idle words; this was the way he worked. He made sure that people understood what was to be done and supported them in doing it.

Empowerment Beyond the Workplace

Empowerment need not be limited to the workplace. Some members of our own consulting team have been working intensely with unemployed people in inner-city areas. For example, a mother of three, who, after years of feeling powerless when dealing with external authorities such as the church, teachers, and doctors, realized that

> . . . it is not us and them. We are all us. I allow myself to be disempowered. Once I realized this I could accept my own responsibility in managing my life. If I sat back, nothing would happen. If I did something, anything could happen. If people did things I didn't like or understand, rather than moan, I now ask why? I demand to be involved. My life is too precious to let someone else take responsibility for it.

Another single parent in the same community, after many years in mental hospitals, refused to live a life dependent on drugs or doctors. She drew on her own resources, determined to take responsibility for her own life. She now runs a voluntary project for people who suffer in a similar way. By helping and managing herself, she not only empowered herself but also found a way to help others to do the same.

There are numerous similar examples—the fourteen-year-old boy, written off by teachers, who saw life as a challenge rather than a threat and recently became top of his college class in stage management; the community members in Belfast who, in the midst of anger and violence, are creating an education center in a rundown house; the prisoner serving a life sentence who became a world-renowned sculptor and writer. These are all people who, against the odds, have made it or are making it. They are people who have drawn on their inner resources to manage their own life. They are people working together, reaching not for the stars, but to live and manage their life in creative ways.

A New Type of Leadership

The leaders of tomorrow will be those people who can create environments in which others feel empowered. This is the essence of good leadership. John Harvey-Jones, ex-chairman of ICI, writes in his book, *Making It Happen: Reflections on Leadership*:

> Business leadership is itself an honorable, testing, imaginative, and creative job. It is not just about the creation of wealth, it is about the creation of a better world for tomorrow and the building and growing of people [1988, p. 262].

He believes that today's generation of independent-minded individuals will stay only with a company that treats them with the highest degree of self-respect. This means that leaders must also be truthful to themselves. He continues on to say that "the most difficult task of the manager is ruthless intellectual honesty about his own skills, weaknesses, and motives"

(1988, p. 262). "Ruthless" for him does not mean climbing over colleagues and competitors in the desperate search for material advantage. It means unflinching self-criticism.

Similar sentiments were recently expressed by Colin Marshall of British Airways:

> Emperors rule; leaders motivate. . . . [They] hold their job by what they inspire their associates to do, not by the diktats they issue. . . .
>
> Our scarcest natural resource is leadership. Not the leadership which adorns itself in fuss and feathers, but that which can get people to do things they did not know they could do. Leadership which depends not on panoply and pageantry, but on an understanding of and caring about the concerns of people [Marshall, 1984].

Another leader who puts the issue of individual growth high on his agenda is the president of a New York high-tech corporation with whom we have worked:

> I want us to create a climate where at the end of a person's career with us they will feel moved to say: "I have used my life with the company in a worthwhile way. Not only was it a good company to work for, but I grew as a human being—through this experience I am a better person in myself."

As well as reconsidering the role of the leader, we also need to reconsider who the leaders are. The conventional idea of the leader is the person at the top of the hierarchical apex, the one who sets a tone to the others who follow, the one who "shows the way." But leadership can come in many different forms.

In the team-role model developed by Belbin (1981) the conventional leader is normally considered to be a person with characteristics of either the shaper or the chairman. These are certainly roles that direct the team in its work toward a goal, but the other roles lead in other ways. The original thinker leads the generation of ideas, the team worker leads the facilitation of the team process, the monitor-evaluator leads the testing of ideas, and the completer-finisher leads ongoing day-to-day work on a project.

The leadership qualities of these and of the other roles are essential if the team is to function at its maximum. If the person performing the role of monitor-evaluator, for example, is not able to help the rest of the team feel empowered, then he or she will not be able to carry out this role effectively. Others may not listen to this person; they may feel threatened by his or her critiques and withdraw, or they may not trust and value their own qualities and abilities.

As much as we need to rethink our ideas on who is creative and who is a manager, we also need to reframe our notion of leadership. Too easily, we see leadership in other people and not the leadership in ourselves, the leadership that we can offer. Yet there is leadership within every person. That leadership comes from an attitude of mind, not necessarily from the qualifications we have or our position. Leaders "show the way," and this is something we are each capable of.

What the world needs now is not just leaders in the conventional sense but people who are willing to show the way—people who can empower themselves, take responsibility for their lives and the world they live in, and create an environment that allows others to feel empowered. Such leaders do not have to be at the top of the hierarchy; they can come from all levels and all walks of life. In this sense, Gandhi, Mother Teresa, and Bob Geldof are models of leadership as much as are the presidents of corporations and countries.

There is no "right" formula for this new type of leader. Some will be charismatic, while others will act more quietly. Some may be strong team players, while others may be strong individualists who appear to "go it alone." Some will be pushy, while others will guide from behind. Some will be emotionally oriented and others, more logical and analytical. Some will be introverted and some, highly extroverted. Some will lead consciously; others will be surprised by the fact that they are seen as leaders.

What the new leaders must share is not a new outer style

as much as a new inner style. They will understand their own motivations as much as what needs to be done. They will bring more of their own inner truth to what they do. They will be people finding the courage to stand for what they value. They will be people who understand that true authority lies in that quiet voice in their heart. They will be people sharing their own learnings and visions, people encouraging others to become true to their own inner voice so that together we can guide ourselves through these extraordinary times.

Marilyn Ferguson sums it up succinctly in her book *The Aquarian Conspiracy*:

> Plato once said that the human race would have no rest from its evils until philosophers became kings or kings became philosophers. Perhaps there is another option, as increasing numbers of people are assuming leadership of their own lives. They become their own central power. As the Scandinavian proverb says, "In each of us there is a king. Speak to him and he will come forth" [1987, p. 239].

AFTERWORD

None of the ideas in this book are new. Some of them may seem new when we first come across them, but on deeper reflection, we often find that they resonate with our own personal intimations and inner knowing. They are things we already know.

We know the world is changing faster, presenting us all with new and profound challenges. We know that past ways of dealing with problems are no longer adequate and that our current attitudes seem to lead to insane solutions. We know our values have to change.

We know we could be more creative than we are. We know that the process of creativity is mysterious and that we cannot force it to happen. We know we can get stuck in the way we see things and how much this limits our behavior. We know we need to be more open minded.

We know that it can be difficult to cope with the pressures of life, and that we must manage ourselves better. We know that we need to learn more about ourselves and that there is a wise voice within each of us, although we do not always trust it. We know that we all have deeper needs and values that we sometimes do not listen to. We know that we want peace of mind. We know that we need to value others and their differences. And we know we cannot achieve these aims on our own.

We also know we are not perfect. We easily forget that we know these things.

Yet these inner knowings are all common sense. They are born of our experience of life. From childhood onward, at home and at work, from the depths of our sufferings to the heights of our joys, we are learning about life. And behind all these learnings are common truths. They are our common sense.

Unfortunately, we often do not believe in ourselves enough to trust our common sense. The conventional wisdom of society conspires against this inner knowing. It would have us believe in a world of fantasy and illusion. We doubt our selves. We keep secret what we know within.

But the truth is out. There is no secret. Our inner knowing is a wisdom we all share. And like all wisdom, it is very simple—tell the truth, take time, listen, honor your feelings, respect others, trust yourself, act with courage, and have fun.

It is the wisdom of the child, brought alive so beautifully by these words of Robert Fulghum:

> Most of what I really need to know about how to live, and what to do, and how to be, I learned in kindergarten. Wisdom was not at the top of the graduate school mountain, but there in the sandbox at nursery school. These are the things I learned: share everything; play fair; don't hit people; put things back where you found them; clean up your own mess; don't take things that aren't yours; say you're sorry when you hurt somebody; wash your hands before you eat. . . .
>
> Warm cookies and cold milk are good for you; live a balanced life; learn some and think some and draw and paint and sing and dance and play and work everyday some; take a nap every afternoon; when you go out into the world, watch for traffic; hold hands and stick together; be aware of wonder. . . .
>
> Think of what a better world it would be if we all—the whole world—had cookies and milk about 3 o'clock every afternoon and then lay down with our blankets for a nap, or if we had a basic policy in our nation and other nations to always put things back where we found them and cleaned up our own messes. And it is still true, no matter how old you are, when you go out into the world, it is best to hold hands and stick together [1989, pp. 6–7].

REFERENCES

Beckett, S. T. Address to the Institute of Directors Conference, London, England, November 11, 1984.

Beer, S. *Platform for Change.* West Sussex, England: John Wiley & Sons, 1975.

Belbin, R. M. *Management Teams: Why They Succeed or Fail.* London: Heinemann, 1981.

Brown, M. *The Dinosaur Strain: The Survivor's Guide to Personal and Business Success.* Shaftesbury, England: Element Books, 1988.

Emerson, R. W. "Self-Reliance." In Edward W. Emerson (ed.), *The Complete Works of Ralph Waldo Emerson.* New York: AMS Pr., Inc. 1903–1904.

Ferguson, M. *The Aquarian Conspiracy: Personal and Social Transformation in Our Time.* Los Angeles: Tarcher, 1987.

Fulghum, R. *All I Really Need to Know I Learned in Kindergarten.* New York: Villard, 1989.

Goldberg, P. *The Intuitive Edge: Understanding and Developing Intuition.* Los Angeles: Tarcher, 1983.

Harvey-Jones, J. *Making It Happen: Reflections on Leadership.* London: Collins, 1988.

Kelly, M. "Revolution in the Marketplace." *Utne Reader*, Jan./Feb. 1989, pp. 54–62.

Kilmann, R. H. *Beyond the Quick Fix: Managing Five Tracks to Organizational Success.* San Francisco: Jossey-Bass, 1984.

Kinsman, F. *The New Agenda.* London: Stuart, 1983.

Lynch, J. J. *The Language of the Heart: The Body's Response to Human Dialogue.* New York: Basic Books, 1985.

MacNulty, W. K. "UK Social Change Through a Wide-Angle Lens." *Futures*, Aug. 1985, pp. 331–347.

Marshall, C. Address to the Institute of Directors Conference, London, England, November 11, 1984.

Maslow, A. *The Farther Reaches of Human Nature.* New York: Viking, 1976.

Morgan, G. *Images of Organization.* Newbury Park, Calif.: Sage, 1986.

Morgan, G. *Riding the Waves of Change: Developing Managerial Competencies for a Turbulent World.* San Francisco: Jossey-Bass, 1988.

Naisbitt, J., and Aburdene, P. *Re-Inventing the Corporation.* New York: Warner, 1985.

Nixon, P.G.F. "Stress and the Cardiovascular System." *Practitioner*, 1982, 226, 1589–1598.

Peters, T. *Thriving on Chaos: Handbook for a Management Revolution.* London: Macmillan, 1987.

Ray, M., and Myers, R. *Creativity in Business.* Garden City, N.Y.: Doubleday, 1986.

Schwartz, T. "Acceleration Syndrome: Does Everyone Live in the Fast Lane Nowadays?" *Vanity Fair*, Oct. 1988.

Sculley, J., with Byrne, J. A. *Odyssey.* New York: HarperCollins, 1987.

Staubli, R. "Human Development: A Crucial Prerequisite for the Efficiency of a Company in a Changing Environment." Fourth European Symposium on Long-Term Questions of the Future, GDI Institute, Rüschlikon, Switzerland, July 3–5, 1986.

Yankelovich, D. *New Rules: Searching for Self-Fulfillment in a World Turned Upside Down.* New York: Random House, 1981.